SEP 2 2 2016

S0-CFF-994

Also by C. K. Williams

Selected Later Poems

3 0053 01245 6110

Farrar, Straus and Giroux *New York*

C. K. Williams

Selected Later Poems

Farrar, Straus and Giroux

18 West 18th Street, New York 10011

Copyright © 2015 by C. K. Williams

All rights reserved

Printed in the United States of America

First edition, 2015

Library of Congress Cataloging-in-Publication Data

Williams, C. K. (Charles Kenneth), 1936–

    [Poems. Selections]

    Selected later poems / C. K. Williams. — First edition.

      pages ; cm

    ISBN 978-0-374-26114-6 (hardback) — ISBN 978-0-374-71372-0 (e-book)

    1. Title.

PS3573.I4483 A6 2015

811'.54—dc23

                                   2015005011

Designed by Quemadura

Farrar, Straus and Giroux books may be purchased for educational, business, or promotional use. For information on bulk purchases, please contact the Macmillan Corporate and Premium Sales Department at 1-800-221-7945, extension 5442, or write to specialmarkets@macmillan.com.

www.fsgbooks.com

www.twitter.com/fsgbooks

www.facebook.com/fsgbooks

10 9 8 7 6 5 4 3 2 1

for

Catherine

Jed

Jessie and Michael

Owen Sully and Turner

Always all

Contents

From *The Singing* (2003)

From *Wait* (2010)

From *Writers Writing Dying* (2012)

From *All at Once* (2014)

New Poems (2015)

From
The
Vigil

(1997)

The Neighbor

Her five horrid, deformed little dogs, who incessantly yap on the roof under my window;
her cats, god knows how many, who must piss on her rugs—her landing's a sickening reek;
her shadow, once, fumbling the chain on her door, then the door slamming fearfully shut:
only the barking, and the music, jazz, filtering as it does day and night into the hall.

The time it was Chris Connor singing "Lush Life," how it brought back my college sweetheart,
my first real love, who, till I left her, played the same record, and, head on my shoulder,
hand on my thigh, sang sweetly along, of regrets and depletions she was too young for,
as I was too young, later, to believe in her pain: it startled, then bored, then repelled me.

My starting to fancy she'd ended up in the first firetrap in the Village, that my neighbor was
    her;
my thinking we'd meet, recognize one another, become friends, that I'd accomplish a penance;
my seeing her—it wasn't her—at the mailbox, gray-yellow hair, army pants under a night-
    gown:
turning away, hiding her ravaged face in her hands, muttering an inappropriate "Hi."

Sometimes, there are frightening goings-on in the stairwell, a man shouting *Shut up!*
the dogs frantically snarling, claws scrabbling, then her, her voice, hoarse, harsh, hollow,
almost only a tone, incoherent, a note, a squawk, bone on metal, metal gone molten,
calling them back, Come back, darlings; come back, dear ones, my sweet angels, come back.

Medea she was, next time I saw her, sorceress, tranced, ecstatic, stock-still on the sidewalk,
ragged coat hanging agape, passersby flowing around her, her mouth torn suddenly open,
as though in a scream, silently though, as though only in her brain or breast had it erupted:
a cry so pure, practiced, detached, it had no need of a voice or could no longer bear one.

These invisible links that allure, these transfigurations even of anguish that hold us:
the girl, my old love, the last, lost time I saw her, when she came to find me at a party:
her drunkenly stumbling, falling, sprawling, skirt hiked, eyes veined red, swollen with tears;
her shame, her dishonor; my ignorant, arrogant coarseness; my secret pride, my turning away.

Still life on a rooftop: dead trees in barrels, a bench, broken; dogs, excrement, sky.
What pathways through pain, what junctures of vulnerability, what crossings and counterings?
Too many lives in our lives already, too many chances for sorrow, too many unaccounted-for
    pasts.
Behold me, the god of frenzied, inexhaustible love says, rising in bloody splendor: *Behold me!*

Her making her way down the littered vestibule stairs, one agonized step at a time;
my holding the door, her crossing the fragmented tiles, faltering at the step to the street,
droning, not looking at me, "Can you help me?" taking my arm, leaning lightly against me;
her wavering step into the world, her whispering, "Thanks, love," lightly, lightly against me.

Dominion: Depression

I don't know what day or year of their secret cycle this blazing golden afternoon might be,
but out in the field in a shrub hundreds of pairs of locusts are locked in a slow sexual seizure.

Hardly more animate than the few leaves they haven't devoured, they seethe like a single being,
limbs, antennas, and wings all tangled together as intricately as a layer of neurons.

Always the neat, tight, gazeless helmet, the exoskeleton burnished like half-hardened glue;
always the abdomen twitched deftly under or aside, the skilled rider, the skillfully ridden.

One male, though, has somehow severed a leg, it sways on the spike of a twig like a harp:
he lunges after his female, tilts, falls; the mass horribly shudders, shifts, realigns.

So dense, so hard, so immersed in their terrible need to endure, so unlike me but like me,
why do they seem such a denial, why do I feel if I plunged my hand in among them I'd die?

This must be what god thinks, beholding his ignorant, obstinate, libidinally maniacal off-spring:
wanting to stop them, to keep them from being so much an image of his impotence or his will.

How divided he is from his creation: even here near the end he sees moving towards him
a smaller, sharper, still more gleaming something, extracting moist matter from a skull.

No more now: he waits, fists full of that mute, oily, crackling, crystalline broil,
then he feels at last the cool wingbeat of the innocent void moving in again over the world.

Fragment

This time the holdup man didn't know a video-sound camera hidden up in a corner
was recording what was before it or more likely he didn't care, opening up with his pistol,
not saying a word, on the clerk you see blurredly falling and you hear—I keep hearing—
crying, "God! God!" in that voice I was always afraid existed within us, the voice that knows
beyond illusion the irrevocability of death, beyond any dream of being not mortally injured—
"You're just going to sleep, someone will save you, you'll wake again, loved ones beside you . . ."
Nothing of that: even torn by the flaws in the tape it was a voice that knew it was dying,
knew it was being—horrible—slaughtered, all that it knew and aspired to instantly voided;
such hopeless, astonished pleading, such overwhelmed, untempered pity for the self dying;
no indignation, no passion for justice, only woe, woe, woe, as he felt himself falling,
even falling knowing already he was dead, and how much I pray to myself I want not, ever,
to know this, how much I want to ask why I must, with such perfect, detailed precision,
know this, this anguish, this agony for a self departing wishing only to stay, to endure,
knowing all the while that, having known, I always will know this torn, singular voice
of a soul calling "God!" as it sinks back through the darkness it came from, canceled, annulled.

My Fly

FOR ERVING GOFFMAN, 1922–1982

One of those great, garishly emerald flies that always look freshly generated from fresh
    excrement
and who maneuver through our airspace with a deft intentionality that makes them seem to
    think,
materializes just above my desk, then vanishes, his dense, abrasive buzz sucked in after him.

I wait, imagine him, hidden somewhere, waiting, too, then think, who knows why, of you—
don't laugh—that he's a messenger from you, or that you yourself (you'd howl at this),
ten years afterwards have let yourself be incarnated as this pestering anti-angel.

Now he, or you, abruptly reappears, with a weightless pounce alighting near my hand.
I lean down close, and though he has to sense my looming presence, he patiently attends,
as though my study of him had become an element of his own observations—maybe it is you!

Joy! To be together, even for a time! Yes, tilt your fuselage, turn it towards the light,
aim the thousand lenses of your eyes back up at me: how I've missed the layers of your
    attention,
how often been bereft without your gift for sniffing out pretentiousness and moral sham.

Why would you come back, though? Was that other radiance not intricate enough to parse?
Did you find yourself in some monotonous century hovering down the tidy queue of creatures
waiting to experience again the eternally unlikely bliss of being matter and extension?

You lift, you land—you're rushed, I know; the interval in all our terminals is much too short.
Now you hurl against the window, skid and jitter on the pane: I open it and step aside
and follow for one final moment of felicity your brilliant, ardent atom swerving through.

Instinct

Although he's apparently the youngest (his little Rasta-beard is barely down and feathers),
most casually connected (he hardly glances at the girl he's with, though she might be his wife),
half-sloshed (or more than half) on picnic whiskey teenaged father, when his little son,
two or so, tumbles from the slide, hard enough to scare himself, hard enough to make him cry,
really cry, not partly cry, not pretend the fright for what must be some scarce attention,
but really let it out, let loudly be revealed the fear of having been so close to real fear,
he, the father, knows just how quickly he should pick the child up, then how firmly hold it,
fit its head into the muscled socket of his shoulder, rub its back, croon and whisper to it,
and finally pull away a little, about a head's length, looking, still concerned, into its eyes,
then smiling, broadly, brightly, as though something had been shared, something of impor-
    tance,
not dreadful, or not very, not at least now that it's past, but rather something . . . funny,
funny, yes, it was funny, wasn't it, to fall and cry like that, though one certainly can under-
    stand,
we've all had glimpses of a premonition of the anguish out there, you're better now, though,
aren't you, why don't you go back and try again, I'll watch you, maybe have another drink,
yes, my son, my love, I'll go back and be myself now: you go be the person you are, too.

My Book, My Book

The book goes fluttering crazily through the space of my room towards the wall like a bird
stunned in mid-flight and impacts and falls not like a bird but more brutally, like a man,
mortally sprawling, spine torn from its sutures, skeletal glue fragmented to crystal and dust.

Submissive, inert, it doesn't as would any other thing wounded shudder, quake, shiver,
act out at least desperate, reflexive attempts towards persistence, endurance, but how could it,
wasn't it shriven already of all but ambition and greed; rote, lame emulations of conviction?

. . . Arrives now to my mind the creature who'll sniff out someday what in this block of
    pretension,
what protein, what atom, might still remain to digest and abstract, transfigure to gist,
what trace of life substance wasn't burned away by the weight of its lovelessness and its sham.

Come, little borer, sting your way in, tunnel more deeply, blast, mine, excavate, drill:
take my book to you, etherealize me in the crunch of your gut; refine me, release me:
let me cling to your brain stem, dissolve in your dreaming: verse, page, quire; devour me,
    devourer.

Symbols

Night, a wildly lashing deluge driving in great gusts over the blind, defeated fields,
the usually stoical larches and pines only the mewling of their suddenly malleable branches;
a wind like a knife that never ceased shrieking except during the stunning volleys of thunder.

By morning, half the hundred pullets in the henhouse had massed in a corner and smothered,
an inert, intricate structure of dulled iridescence and still-distracted, still-frenzied eyes,
the vivid sapphire of daybreak tainted by a vaporous, gorge-swelling fetor.

The tribe of survivors compulsively hammered their angular faces as usual into the trough:
nothing in the world, they were saying, not carnage or dissolution, can bear reflection;
the simplest acts of being, they were saying, can obliterate all, all madness, all mourning.

2. GUITAR

For long decades the guitar lay disregarded in its case, unplucked and untuned,
then one winter morning, the steam heat coming on hard, the maple neck swelling again,
the sixth, gravest string, weary of feeling itself submissively tugged to and fro

over the ivory lip of the bridge, could no longer bear the tension preceding release,
and, with a faint thud and a single, weak note like a groan stifled in a fist, it gave way,
its portions curling agonizingly back on themselves like sundered segments of worm.

. . . The echoes abruptly decay; silence again, the other strings still steadfast, still persevering,
still feeling the music potent within them, their conviction of timelessness only confirmed,
of being essential, elemental, like earth, fire, air, from which all beauty must be evolved.

3. OWL

The just-fledged baby owl a waiter has captured under a tree near the island restaurant
seems strangely unfazed to be on display on a formica table, though she tilts ludicrously,
all her weight on one leg as though she had merely paused in her lift towards departure.

Immobile except for her constantly swiveling head, she unpredictably fixes her gaze,
clicking from one far focus to another—sea, tree, sky, sometimes it seems even star—
but never on hand or eye, no matter how all in the circle around her chirp and cajole.

Thus the gods once, thus still perhaps gods: that scrutiny densely grained as granite,
the rotation calibrated on chromium bearings; dilation, contraction; wrath, disdain, and
remove ...
But oh, to be slipping ever backwards in time, the savage memories, the withheld cry!

4. DOG

Howl after pitiful, aching howl: an enormous, efficiently muscular doberman pinscher
has trapped itself in an old-fashioned phone booth, the door closed firmly upon it,
but when someone approaches to try to release it, the howl quickens and descends,

and if someone in pity dares anyway lean on and crack open an inch the obstinate hinge,
the quickened howl is a snarl, the snarl a blade lathed in the scarlet gape of the gullet,
and the creature powers itself towards that sinister slit, ears flattened, fangs flashing,

the way, caught in the deepest, most unknowing cell of itself, heart's secret, heart's wound,
decorous usually, seemly, though starving now, desperate, will turn nonetheless, raging,
ready to kill, or die, to stay where it is, to maintain itself just as it is, decorous, seemly.

5. FIRE

The plaster had been burned from the studs, the two-by-four joists were eaten with char;
ceilings smoke-blackened, glass fragments and foul, soaked rags of old rug underfoot:
even the paint on the outside brick had bubbled in scabs and blisters and melted away.

Though the fire was ostensibly out, smoke still drifted up through cracks in the floor,
and sometimes a windowsill or a door frame would erupt in pale, insidious flames,
subtle in the darkness, their malignancies masked in blushes of temperate violet and rose.

Like love it was, love ill and soiled; like affection, affinity, passion, misused and consumed;
warmth betrayed, patience exhausted, distorted, all evidence of kindness now unkindness . . .
Yet still the hulk, the gutted carcass; fuming ash and ember; misery and shame.

6. DAWN

Herds of goats puttering by on the rock-strewn path in what sounded like felt slippers;
before that (because the sudden awareness of it in sleep always came only after it passed),
the church bell, its cry in the silence like a swell of loneliness, then loneliness healed.

The resonant *clock* of the fisherman's skiff being tethered to the end of the jetty;
the sad, repetitive smack of a catch of squid being slapped onto a slab of concrete;
the waves, their eternal morning torpor, the cypress leaning warily back from the shore.

A voice from a hill or another valley, expanding, concretizing like light, falling, fading,
then a comic grace note, the creak of rickety springs as someone turns in their bed:
so much beginning, and now, sadness nearly, to think one might not even have known!

7. WIG

The bus that won't arrive this freezing, bleak, pre-Sabbath afternoon must be Messiah;
the bewigged woman, pacing the sidewalk, furious, seething, can be only the mystic She-
    kinah,
the presence of God torn from Godhead, chagrined, abandoned, longing to rejoin, reunite.

The husband in his beard and black hat, pushing a stroller a step behind her as she stalks?
The human spirit, which must slog through such degrading tracts of slush and street-filth,
bound forever to its other, no matter how incensed she may be, how obliviously self-absorbed.

And the child, asleep, serene uncaring in the crank and roar of traffic, his cheeks afire,
ladders of snowy light leaping and swirling above him, is what else but psyche, holy psyche,
always only now just born, always now just waking, to the ancient truths of knowledge, suffer-
    ing, loss.

8. GARDEN

A garden I usually never would visit; oaks, roses, the scent of roses I usually wouldn't remark
but do now, in a moment for no reason suddenly unlike any other, numinous, limpid,
   abundant,
whose serenity lifts and enfolds me, as a swirl of breeze lifts the leaves and enfolds them.

Nothing ever like this, not even love, though there's no need to measure, no need to compare:
for once not to be waiting, to be in the world as time moves through and across me,
to exult in this fragrant light given to me, in this flow of warmth given to me and the world.

Then, on my hand beside me on the bench, something, I thought somebody else's hand,
   alighted;
I flinched it off, and saw—sorrow!—a warbler, gray, black, yellow, in flight already away.
It stopped near me in a shrub, though, and waited, as though unstartled, as though unafraid,

as though to tell me my reflex of fear was no failure, that if I believed I had lost something,
I was wrong, because nothing can be lost, of the self, of a lifetime of bringing forth selves.
Then it was gone, its branch springing back empty: still oak, though, still rose, still world.

Realms

Often I have thought that after my death, not in death's void as we usually think it,
but in some simpler after-realm of the mind, it will be given to me to transport myself
through all space and all history, to behold whatever and converse with whomever I wish.

Sometimes I might be an actual presence, a traveler listening at the edge of the crowd;
at other times I'd have no physical being; I'd move unseen but seeing through palace or slum.
Sophocles, Shakespeare, Bach! Grandfathers! *Homo erectus*! The universe bursting into being!

Now, though, as I wake, caught by some imprecise longing, you in the darkness beside me,
your warmth flowing gently against me, it comes to me that in all my after-death doings,
I see myself as alone, always alone, and I'm suddenly stranded, forsaken, desperate, lost.

To propel myself through those limitless reaches without you! Never! Be with me, come!
Babylon, Egypt, Lascaux, the new seas boiling up life; Dante, Delphi, Magyars, and Mayans!
Wait, though, it must be actually you, not my imagination of you, however real: for myself,

mind would suffice, no matter if all were one of time's terrible toys, but I must have you,
as you are, the unquenchable fire of your presence, otherwise death truly would triumph.
Quickly, never mind death, never mind mute, oblivious, onrushing time: wake, hold me!

Storm

Another burst of the interminable, intermittently torrential dark afternoon downpour,
and the dozens of tirelessly garrulous courtyard sparrows stop hectoring each other
and rush to park under a length of cornice endearingly soiled with decades of wing grease.

The worst summer in memory, thermal inversion, smog, swelter, intimations of global warming;
though the plane trees still thrust forth buds as though innocent April were just blooming,
last week's tentative pre-green leaflings are already woefully charred with heat and pollution.

Thunder far off, benign, then closer, slashes of lightning, a massive, concussive unscrolling,
an answering tremor in the breast, the exaltation at sharing a planet with this, then sorrow;
that we really might strip it of all but the bare wounded rock lumbering down its rote rail.

A denser veil of clouds now, another darkening downlash, the wind rises, the sparrows scatter,
the leaves quake, and Oh, I throw myself this way, the trees say, then that way, I tremble,
I moan, and still you don't understand the absence I'll be in the void of unredeemable time.

. . . Twelve suns, the prophecies promise, twelve vast suns of purification will mount the
     horizon,
to scorch, sear, burn away, then twelve cosmic cycles of rain: no tree left, no birdsong,
only the vigilant, acid waves, vindictively scouring themselves again and again on no shore.

Imagine then the emergence: Oh, this way, the sky streaked, Oh, that way, with miraculous
     brightness;
imagine us, beginning again, timid and tender, with a million years more this time to evolve,
an epoch more on all fours, stricken with shame and repentance, before we fire our forges.

The Bed

Beds squalling, squealing, muffled in hush; beds pitching, leaping, immobile as mountains;
beds wide as a prairie, strait as a gate, as narrow as the plank of a ship to be walked.

I squalled, I squealed, I swooped and pitched; I covered my eyes and fell from the plank.

Beds proud, beds preening, beds timid and tense; vanquished beds wishing only to vanquish;
neat little beds barely scented and dented, beds so disused you cranked them to start them.

I admired, sang praises, flattered, adored: I sighed and submitted, solaced, comforted, cranked.

Procrustean beds with consciences sharpened like razors slicing the darkness above you;
beds like the labors of Hercules, stables and serpents; Samson blinded, Noah in horror.

Blind with desire, I wakened in horror, in toil, in bondage, my conscience in tatters.

Beds sobbing, beds sorry, beds pleading, beds mournful with histories that amplified yours,
so you knelled through their dolorous echoes as through the depths of your own dementias.

I echoed, I knelled, I sobbed and repented, I bandaged the wrists, sighed for embryos lost.

A nation of beds, a cosmos, then, how could it still happen the bed at the end of the world,
as welcoming as the world, ark, fortress, light and delight, the other beds all forgive, forgiving.

A bed that sang through the darkness and woke in song as though world itself had just wakened;
two beds fitted together as one; bed of peace, patience, arrival, bed of unwaning ardor.

Grace

Almost as good as her passion, I'll think, almost as good as her presence, her physical grace,
almost as good as making love with her, I'll think in my last aching breath before last,
my glimpse before last of the light, were her good will and good wit, the steadiness of her
   affections.

Almost, I'll think, sliding away on my sleigh of departure, the rind of my consciousness
   thinning,
the fear of losing myself, of—worse—losing her, subsiding as I think, hope it must,
almost as good as her beauty, her glow, was the music of her thought, her voice and laughter.

Almost as good as kissing her, being kissed back, I hope I'll have strength still to think,
was watching her as she worked or read, was beholding her selfless sympathy for son, friend,
   sister,
even was feeling her anger, sometimes, rarely, lift against me, then be forgotten, put aside.

Almost, I'll think, as good as our unlikely coming together was our constant, mostly unspoken
   debate
as to whether good in the world was good in itself, or (my side) only the absence of evil:
no need to say how much how we lived was shaped by her bright spirit, her humor and hope.

Almost as good as living at all—improbable gift—was watching her once cross our room,
the reflections of night rain she'd risen to close the window against flaring across her,
doubling her light, then feeling her come back to bed, reaching to find and embrace me,

as I'll hope she'll be there to embrace me as I sail away on that last voyage out of myself,
that last passage out of her presence, though her presence, I'll think, will endure,
as firmly as ever, as good even now, I'll think in that lull before last, almost as ever.

Thirst

Here was my relation with the woman who lived all last autumn and winter day and night
on a bench in the Hundred and Third Street subway station until finally one day she vanished:

we regarded each other, scrutinized one another: me shyly, obliquely, trying not to be furtive;
she boldly, unblinkingly, even pugnaciously; wrathfully even, when her bottle was empty.

I was frightened of her, I felt like a child, I was afraid some repressed part of myself
would go out of control and I'd be forever entrapped in the shocking seethe of her stench.

Not excrement merely, not merely surface and orifice going unwashed, rediffusion of rum:
there was will in it, and intention, power and purpose; a social, ethical rage and rebellion.

. . . Despair, too, though, grief, loss: sometimes I'd think I should take her home with me,
bathe her, comfort her, dress her: she wouldn't have wanted me to, I would think.

Instead I'd step into my train: how rich, I would think, is the lexicon of our self-absolving;
how enduring our bland, fatal assurance that reflection is righteousness being accomplished.

The dance of our glances, the clash; pulling each other through our perceptual punctures;
then holocaust, holocaust: host on host of ill, injured presences squandered, consumed.

Her vigil, somewhere, I know, continues: her occupancy, her absolute, faithful attendance;
the dance of our glances: challenge, abdication, effacement; the perfume of our consternation.

From
Repair

(1999)

Ice

That astonishing thing that happens when you crack a needle awl into a block of ice:
the way a perfect section through it crazes into gleaming fault lines, fractures, facets;
dazzling silvery deltas that in one too-quick-to-capture instant madly complicate the cosmos of
    its innards.
Radiant now with spines and spikes, aggressive barbs of glittering light, a treasure hoard of light,
when you stab it again it comes apart in nearly equal segments, both faces grainy, gnawed at,
    dull.

An icehouse was a dark, low place of raw, unpainted wood,
always dank and black with melting ice.
There was sawdust and sawdust's tantalizing, half-sweet odor, which, so cold, seemed to pierce
    directly to the brain.
You'd step onto a low-roofed porch, someone would materialize,
take up great tongs and with precise, placating movements like a lion-tamer's slide an ice-block
    from its row.

Take the awl yourself now, thrust, and when the block splits do it again, yet again;
watch it disassemble into smaller fragments, crystal after fissured crystal.
Or if not the puncturing pick, try to make a metaphor, like Kafka's frozen sea within:
take into your arms the cake of actual ice, make a figure of its ponderous inertness,
of how its quickly wetting chill against your breast would frighten you and make you let it drop.

Imagine how even if it shattered and began to liquefy
the hope would still remain that if you quickly gathered up the slithery, perversely skittish chips,
they might be refrozen and the mass reconstituted, with precious little of its brilliance lost,
just this lucent shimmer on the rough, raised grain of water-rotten floor,
just this single drop, as sweet and warm as blood, evaporating on your tongue.

Archetypes

Often before have our fingers touched in sleep or half-sleep and enlaced,
often I've been comforted through a dream by that gently sensitive pressure,
but this morning, when I woke your hand lay across mine in an awkward,
unfamiliar position so that it seemed strangely external to me, removed;
an object whose precise weight, volume, and form I'd never remarked:
its taut, resistant skin, dense muscle pads, the subtle, complex structure,
with delicately elegant chords of bone aligned like columns in a temple.

Your fingers began to move then, in brief, irregular tensions and releasings;
it felt like your hand was trying to hold some feathery, fleeting creature,
then you suddenly, fiercely, jerked it away, rose to your hands and knees,
and stayed there, palms flat on the bed, hair tangled down over your face,
until with a coarse sigh almost like a snarl you abruptly let yourself fall
and lay still, your hands drawn tightly to your chest, your head turned away,
forbidden to me, I thought, by whatever had raised you to that defiant crouch.

I waited, hoping you'd wake, turn, embrace me, but you stayed in yourself,
and I felt again how separate we all are from one another, how even our passions,
which seem to embody unities outside of time, heal only the most benign divisions,
that for our more abiding, ancient terrors we each have to find our own valor.
You breathed more softly now, though; I took heart, touched against you,
and, as though nothing had happened, you opened your eyes, smiled at me,
and murmured—how almost startling to hear you in your real voice—"Sleep, love."

After Auschwitz

We'd wanted to make France
but by dusk we knew we wouldn't,
so in a Bavarian town
just off the autobahn,
we found a room, checked in,
and went out to look around.

The place was charming: hushed,
narrow, lamp-lit streets,
half-timbered houses,
a dark-stoned church
and medieval bridges
over a murmuring river.

I didn't sleep well, though,
and in the morning, early,
I took another stroll
and was surprised to realize
that all of it, houses,
bridges, all except

as far as I could tell
the sleeping church, were deft
replicas of what
they must have been before
the war, before the Allied
bombers flattened them.

At Auschwitz, there was nothing
I hadn't imagined beforehand.
I'd been through it in my mind
so much, so often, I felt
only unutterably weary.
All that shocked me was

to find the barracks and bleak
paths unoccupied,
and the gas and torture chambers,
and the crematoria;
so many silent spaces,
bereft, like schools in summer.

Now, in a pleasant square,
I came on a morning market;
farmers, tents and trucks,
much produce, flowers,
the people prosperous,
genial, ruddy, chatty,

and it was then there arose
before me again the barbed
wire and the bales of hair,
the laboratories and
the frozen ash. I thought
of Primo Levi, reciting

Dante to the all but dead,
then, I don't know why,
of the Jewish woman, Masha,

of whom Levi tells
how, when she'd escaped,
been informed on, caught,

and now was to be hanged
before the other prisoners,
someone called out to her,
"Masha, are you all right?"
and she'd answered, answered, answered,
"I'm always all right."

A village like a stage set,
a day's drive back
that other place which always
now everywhere on earth
will be the other place
from where one finds oneself.

Not risen from its ruins
but caught in them forever,
it demands of us how
we'll situate this so
it doesn't sunder us
between forgivenesses

we have no right to grant,
and a reticence
perhaps malignant, heard
by nothing that exists,
yet which endures, a scar,
a broken cry, within.

The Dress

In those days, those days which exist for me only as the most elusive memory now,
when often the first sound you'd hear in the morning would be a storm of birdsong,
then the soft clop of the hooves of the horse hauling a milk wagon down your block

and the last sound at night as likely as not would be your father pulling up in his car,
having worked late again, always late, and going heavily down to the cellar, to the furnace,
to shake out the ashes and damp the draft before he came upstairs to fall into bed;

in those long-ago days, women, my mother, my friends' mothers, our neighbors,
all the women I knew, wore, often much of the day, what were called "housedresses,"
cheap, printed, pulpy, seemingly purposefully shapeless light cotton shifts

that you wore over your nightgown, and, when you had to go to look for a child,
hang wash on the line, or run down to the grocery store on the corner, under a coat,
the twisted hem of the nightgown, always lank and yellowed, dangling beneath.

More than the curlers some of the women seemed constantly to have in their hair,
in preparation for some great event, a ball, one would think, that never came to pass;
more than the way most women's faces not only were never made up during the day,

but seemed scraped, bleached, and, with their plucked eyebrows, scarily masklike;
more than all that it was those dresses that made women so unknowable and forbidding,
adepts of enigmas to which men could have no access, and boys no conception.

Only later would I see the dresses also as a proclamation: that in your dim kitchen,
your laundry, your bleak concrete yard, what you revealed of yourself was a fabulation;
your real sensual nature, veiled in those sexless vestments, was utterly your dominion.

In those days, one hid much else, as well: grown men didn't embrace one another,
unless someone had died, and not always then; you shook hands, or, at a ball game,
thumped your friend's back and exchanged blows meant to be codes for affection;

once out of childhood you'd never again know the shock of your father's whiskers
on your cheek, not until mores at last had evolved, and you could hug another man,
then hold on for a moment, then even kiss (your father's bristles white and stiff now).

What release finally, the embrace: though we were wary—it seemed so audacious—
how much unspoken joy there was in that affirmation of equality and communion,
no matter how much misunderstanding and pain had passed between you by then.

We knew so little in those days, as little as now, I suppose, about healing those hurts:
even the women, in their best dresses, with beads and sequins sewn on the bodices,
even in lipstick and mascara, their hair aflow, could only stand wringing their hands,

begging for peace, while father and son, like thugs, like thieves, like Romans,
simmered and hissed and hated, inflicting sorrows that endured, the worst anyway,
through the kiss and embrace, bleeding from brother to brother into the generations.

In those days there was still countryside close to the city, farms, cornfields, cows;
even not far from our building with its blurred brick and long shadowy hallway
you could find tracts with hills and trees you could pretend were mountains and forests.

Or you could go out by yourself even to a half-block-long empty lot, into the bushes:
like a creature of leaves you'd lurk, crouched, crawling, simplified, savage, alone;
already there was wanting to be simpler, wanting when they called you, never to go back.

Bone

An erratic, complicated shape, like a tool for some obsolete task:

the hip bone and half the gnawed shank of a small, unrecognizable animal on the pavement in
front of the entrance to the museum;

grimy, black with tire dust, soot, the blackness from our shoes, our ink, the grit that sifts out of
our air.

Still, something devoured all but this much, and if you look more closely,

you can see tiny creatures still gnawing at the shreds of decomposing meat, sucking at all but
putrefying bone.

Decades it must be on their scale that they harvest it, dwell and generate and age and die on it.

Where will they transport the essence of it when they're done?

How far beneath the asphalt, sewers, subways, mains, and conduits is the living earth to which
at last they'll once again descend?

Which intellect will register in its neurons the great fortune of this exceptional adventure?
Which poet sing it?

Such sweetness, such savor: luxury, satiety, and no repentance, no regret.

But Maman won't let you keep it.

"Maman, please . . ."

"It's filthy. Drop it. *Drop it! Drop it! Drop it!*"

Droplets

Even when the rain falls relatively hard,
only one leaf at a time of the little tree
you planted on the balcony last year,
then another leaf at its time, and one more,
is set trembling by the constant droplets,

but the rain, the clouds flocked over the city,
you at the piano inside, your hesitant music
mingling with the din of the downpour,
the gush of rivulets loosed from the eaves,
the iron railings and flowing gutters,

all of it fuses in me with such intensity
that I can't help wondering why my longing
to live forever has so abated that it hardly
comes to me anymore, and never as it did,
as regret for what I might not live to live,

but rather as a layering of instants like this,
transient as the mist drawn from the rooftops,
yet emphatic as any note of the nocturne
you practice, and, the storm faltering, fading
into its own radiant passing, you practice again.

House

The way you'd renovate a ruined house, keeping the "shell," as we call it, brick, frame, or stone,
and razing the rest: the inside walls—partitions, we say—then stairs, pipes, wiring, commodes,
saving only . . . no, save nothing this time; take the self-shell down to its emptiness, hollowness, void.

Down to the scabrous plaster, down to the lining bricks with mortar squashed through their joints,
down to the eyeless windows, the forlorn doorless doorways, the sprung joists powdery with rot;
down to the slab of the cellar, the erratically stuccoed foundation, the black earth underneath all.

Down under all to the ancient errors, indolence, envy, pretension, the frailties as though in the gene;
down to where consciousness cries, "Make me new," but pleads as pitiably, "Cherish me as I was."
Down to the swipe of the sledge, the ravaging bite of the pick; rubble, wreckage, vanity: the abyss.

Shoe

A pair of battered white shoes has been left out all night on a sill across the way.
One, the right, has its toe propped against the pane so that it tilts oddly upwards,
and there's an abandon in its attitude, an elevation, that reminds me of a satyr on a vase.

A fleece of summer ivy casts the scene into deep relief, and I see the creature perfectly:
surrounded by his tribe of admiring women, he glances coolly down at his own lifted foot,
caught exactly at the outset of the frenzied leaping which will lift all of them to rapture.

The erotic will diffused directly into matter: you can sense his menacing lasciviousness,
his sensual glaze, his delight in being flagrant, so confidently more than merely mortal,
separate from though hypercritically aware of earthly care, of our so amusing earthly woe.

All that carnal scorn which in his dimension is a fitting emblem for his energy and grace,
but which in our meager world would be hubris, arrogance, compensation for some lack or loss,
or for that passion to be other than we are that with a shock of longing takes me once again.

The Cup

What was going through me at that time of childhood
when my mother drinking her morning coffee would drive me wild with loathing and despair?
Every day, her body hunched with indignation at having had to leave its sleep,
her face without its rouge an almost mortal pale,
she'd stand before the stove and wait until the little turret on the coffeepot subsided,
then she'd fill her cup and navigate her way across the kitchen.

At the table, she'd set the cup down in its saucer, pour in milk, sit,
let out a breath charged with some onerous responsibility I never understood,
and lift the cup again.
There'd be a tiny pause as though she had consciously to synchronize her mouth and hand,
then her lips would lengthen and reach out, prehensile as a primate's tail,
and seem to *grasp* the liquid with the sputtering suctioning of gravity imperfectly annulled.
Then, grimacing as though it were a molten metal she was bringing into herself—
always grimacing, I'd think: did she never know what temperature the stuff would be?—
she'd hold about a spoonful just behind her teeth before she'd slide it thickly down.

Thickly, much too thickly:
she must have changed its gravity in there to some still more viscous, lavalike elixir.
Then there'd be a grateful lowering of her shoulders.
Also then her eyes would lift to focus on a point beyond my head
as though always then a thought had come to her that needed rarer ranges of reflection.
She'd do that twice, all that always twice, and put the coffee down.
In its porcelain cauldron, the military-brownish broth would sway—
was her passion for it going to make it boil again?—and finally come to rest.

. . . As *I* never came to rest, as I had to watch, I knew the interval by heart,

her hand come down to it again, her head lower to it again,

that excruciating suction sound again, her gaze loosening again.

I'd be desperate, wild, my heart would pound.

There was an expression then, "to tell on someone": that was what I craved, to *tell* on her,

to have someone bear witness with me to her awful wrong.

What was I doing to myself? Or she to me?

Oh, surely she to me!

Tree

One vast segment of the tree, the very topmost, blows ceremoniously against a breath of breeze,
patient, sagacious, apparently possessing the wisdom such a union of space, light, and matter
   should.

Just beneath, though grazed by the same barely perceptible zephyr, a knot of leaves quakes
   hectically,
as though trying to convince that more pacific presence above it of its anxieties, its dire
   forebodings.

Now some of the individual spreads that make up the higher, ponderous, stoic portion are
   caught, too,
by a more insistent pressure: their unity disrupted, they sway irrationally; do they, too, sense
   danger?

Harried, quaking, they seem to wonder whether some untoward response will be demanded
   of them,
whether they'll ever graze again upon the ichor with which such benign existences sustain
   themselves.

A calming now, a more solid, gel-like weight of heat in the air, in the tree a tense, tremulous
   subsiding;
the last swelling and flattening of the thousand glittering armadas of sunlight passing through
   the branches.

The tree's negative volume defines it now; the space it contains contained in turn by the un-
   moving warmth,
by duration breathlessly suspended, and, for me, by a languorous sense of being all at once
   pacified, quelled.

Owen: Seven Days

FOR OWEN BURNS,

BORN MARCH 5, 1997

Well here I
go again into my
grandson's eyes

seven days
old and he knows
nothing logic tells me

yet when I
look into his eyes
darkish grayish blue

a whole tone
lighter
than his mother's

I feel myself almost
with a *whoosh*
dragged

into his consciousness
and processed
processed processed

his brows knit
I'm in there now
I don't know

in what form but
his gaze hasn't
faltered an instant

though still his
brows knit and
knit as though to

get just right
what I am no
what I'm thinking

as though to get
what I'm thinking
just exactly right

in perplexity perhaps
his brows knit
once again

perhaps because
of how little
inscrutability

with which the
problem of me
is presented

not "Who are you?"
but more something
like "Why?

Why are you? Out
there? Do you
know?"

then his eyelids
start to flutter
time to sleep

and once again with
something like
another *whoosh*

I'm ejected back
out into my
world

bereft? no
but for an instant
maybe just a little

lonely just a
little desolated
just for a while

utterly confounded
by the sheer
propulsive

force of
being taken
by such love

Gas

Wouldn't it be nice, I think, when the blue-haired lady in the doctor's waiting room bends over the magazine table

and farts, just a little, and violently blushes, wouldn't it be nice if intestinal gas came embodied in visible clouds

so she could see that her really quite inoffensive *pop* had only barely grazed my face before it drifted away?

Besides, for this to have happened now is a nice coincidence because not an hour ago, while we were on our walk,

my dog was startled by a backfire and jumped straight up like a horse bucking and that brought back to me

the stable I worked on weekends when I was twelve and a splendid piebald stallion who whenever he was mounted

would buck just like that, though more hugely, of course, enormous, gleaming resplendent, and the woman,

her face abashedly buried in her *Elle* now, reminded me I'd forgotten that not the least part of my awe

consisted of the fact that with every jump he took the horse would powerfully fart, *fwap*, *fwap*, *fwap*,

something never mentioned in the dozens of books about horses and their riders I devoured in those days.

All that savage grandeur, the steely glinting hooves, the eruptions driven from the creature's mighty innards:

breath stopped, heart stopped, nostrils madly flared, I didn't know if I wanted to break him or be him.

The Nail

Some dictator or other had gone into exile, and now reports were coming about his regime,
the usual crimes, torture, false imprisonment, cruelty, and corruption, but then a detail:
that the way his henchmen had disposed of enemies was by hammering nails into their skulls.
Horror, then, what mind does after horror, after that first feeling that you'll never catch your
   breath,
mind imagines—how not be annihilated by it?—the preliminary tap, feels it in the tendons
   of the hand,
feels the way you do with *your* nail when you're fixing something, making something, shelves,
   a bed;
the first light tap to set the slant, and then the slightly harder tap, to embed the tip a little
   more . . .

No, no more: this should be happening in myth, in stone, or paint, not in reality, not here;
it should be an emblem of itself, not itself, something that would *mean*, not really have to
   happen,
something to go out, expand in implication from that unmoved mass of matter in the breast;
as in the image of an anguished face, in grief for us, not as us as us, us as in a myth, a moral
   tale,
a way to tell the truth that grief is limitless, a way to tell us we must always understand
it's we who do such things, we who set the slant, embed the tip, lift the sledge and drive the
   nail,
drive the nail which is the axis upon which turns the brutal human world upon the world.

The Dance

A middle-aged woman, quite plain, to be polite about it, and somewhat stout, to be more cour-
   teous still,
but when she and the rather good-looking, much younger man she's with get up to dance,
her forearm descends with such delicate lightness, such restrained but confident ardor athwart
   his shoulder,
drawing him to her with such a firm, compelling warmth, and moving him with effortless grace
into the union she's instantly established with the not at all rhythmically solid music in this
   second-rate café,

that something in the rest of us, some doubt about ourselves, some sad conjecture, seems to
   be allayed,
nothing that we'd ever thought of as a real lack, nothing not to be admired or be repentant for,
but something to which we've never adequately given credence,
which might have consoling implications about how we misbelieve ourselves, and so the world,
that world beyond us which so often disappoints, but which sometimes shows us, lovely, what
   we are.

Swifts

Why this much fascination with you, little loves, why this what feels like, oh, hearts,
almost too much exultation in you who set the day's end sky ashimmer with your veerings?
Why this feeling one might stay forever to behold you as you bank, swoop, swerve, soar,
make folds and pleats in evening's velvet, and pierce and stitch, dissect, divide,
cast up slopes which hold a beat before they fall away into the softening dusk?
That such fragile beings should concoct such sky-long lifting bends across the roofs,
as though human work counted for as little as your quickly dimming intersecting cries.

Tiniest dear ones, but chargers, too, gleaming, potent little coursers of the firmament,
smaller surely, lighter, but with that much force, that much insistence and enchantment;
godlings, nearly, cast upon the sky as upon a field of thought until then never thought,
gravity exempting from its weary weight its favorite toy, oh, you, and its delights, you and you,
as you hurl yourself across the tint of sinking sunlight that flows behind you as a wake of gold.
And the final daylight sounds you wing back to your eaves with you to weave into the hush,
then your after-hush which pulses in the sky of memory one last beat more as full dark falls.

Invisible Mending

Three women old as angels,
bent as ancient apple trees,
who, in a storefront window,
with magnifying glasses,
needles fine as hair, and shining
scissors, parted woof from warp
and pruned what would in
human tissue have been sick.

Abrasions, rents and frays,
slits and chars and acid
splashes, filaments that gave
way of their own accord
from the stress of spanning
tiny, trifling gaps, but which
in a wounded psyche
make a murderous maze.

Their hands as hard as horn,
their eyes as keen as steel,
the threads they worked with
must have seemed as thick
as ropes on ships, as cables
on a crane, but still their heads
would lower, their teeth bare
to nip away the raveled ends.

Only sometimes would they
lift their eyes to yours to show
how much lovelier than these twists
of silk and serge the garments
of the mind are, yet how much
more benign their implements
than mind's procedures
of forgiveness and repair.

And in your loneliness you'd notice
how really very gently they'd take
the fabric to its last, with what
solicitude gather up worn edges
to be bound, with what severe
but kind detachment wield
their amputating shears:
forgiveness, and repair.

From
The
Singing

(2003)

The Singing

I was walking home down a hill near our house on a balmy afternoon under the blossoms
Of the pear trees that go flamboyantly mad here every spring with their burgeoning forth

When a young man turned in from a corner singing no it was more of a cadenced shouting
Most of which I couldn't catch I thought because the young man was black speaking black

It didn't matter I could tell he was making his song up which pleased me he was nice-looking
Husky dressed in some style of big pants obviously full of himself hence his lyrical flowing over

We went along in the same direction then he noticed me there almost beside him and "Big"
He shouted-sang "Big" and I thought how droll to have my height incorporated in his song

So I smiled but the face of the young man showed nothing he looked in fact pointedly away
And his song changed "I'm not a nice person" he chanted "I'm not I'm not a nice person"

No menace was meant I gathered no particular threat but he did want to be certain I knew
That if my smile implied I conceived of anything like concord between us I should forget it

That's all nothing else happened his song became indecipherable to me again he arrived
Where he was going a house where a girl in braids waited for him on the porch that was all

No one saw no one heard all the unasked and unanswered questions were left where they were
It occurred to me to sing back "I'm not a nice person either" but I couldn't come up with a tune

Besides I wouldn't have meant it nor he have believed it both of us knew just where we were
In the duet we composed the equation we made the conventions to which we were condemned

Sometimes it feels even when no one is there that someone something is watching and listening
Someone to rectify redo remake this time again though no one saw nor heard no one was there

Bialystok, or Lvov

A squalid wayside inn, reeking barn-brewed vodka,
cornhusk cigarettes that cloy like acrid incense
in a village church, kegs of rotten, watered wine,
but then a prayer book's worn-thin pages,
and over them, as though afloat in all that fetidness,
my great-grandfather's disembodied head.

Cacophonous drunkenness, lakes of vomit
and oceans of obscenities; the smallpox-pocked
salacious peasant faces whose carious breath
clots one's own; and violence, the scorpion-
brutal violence of nothing else, to do, to have,
then the prayers again, that tormented face,

its shattered gaze, and that's all I have
of whence I came, of where the blood came from
that made my blood, and the tale's not even mine,
I have it from a poet, the Russian-Jewish then
Israeli Bialik, and from my father speaking of
his father's father dying in his miserable tavern,

in a fight, my father said, with berserk Cossacks,
but my father fabulated, so I omit all that,
and share the poet's forebears, because mine
only wanted to forget their past of poverty
and pogrom, so said nothing, or perhaps
where someone came from, a lost name,

otherwise nothing, leaving me less
history than a dog, just the poet's father's
and my great-grandfather's inn, that sty,
the poet called it, that abyss of silence, I'd say,
and that soul, like snow, the poet wrote,
with tears of blood, I'd add, for me and mine.

This Happened

A student, a young woman, in a fourth-floor hallway of her *lycée*,

perched on the ledge of an open window chatting with friends between classes;

a teacher passes and chides her, *Be careful, you might fall*,

almost banteringly chides her, *You might fall*,

and the young woman, eighteen, a girl really, though she wouldn't think that,

as brilliant as she is, first in her class, *and beautiful, too*, she's often told,

smiles back, and leans into the open window, which wouldn't even be open if it were winter,

if it were winter someone would have closed it (*Close it!*)

leans into the window, farther, still smiling, farther and farther,

though it takes less time than this, really an instant, and lets herself fall. *Herself fall.*

A casual impulse, a fancy, never thought of until now, hardly thought of even now . . .

No, more than impulse or fancy, the girl knows what she's doing,

the girl means something, the girl means to *mean*,

because, it occurs to her in that instant, that beautiful or not, bright yes or no,

she's not who she is, *she's not the person she is*, and the reason, she suddenly knows,

is that there's been so much premeditation where she is, so much plotting and planning,

there's hardly a person where she is, or if there is, it's not her, or not wholly her,

it's a self inhabited, lived in by her, and seemingly even as she thinks it

she knows what's been missing: grace, not premeditation but grace,

a kind of being in the world spontaneously, with *grace*.

Weightfully upon me was the world.

Weightfully this self which graced the world yet never wholly itself.

Weightfully this self which weighed upon me,

the release from which is what I desire and what I achieve.

And the girl remembers, in this infinite instant already so many times divided, the grief she felt once, hardly knowing she felt it, to merely inhabit herself.

Yes, the girl falls, absurd to fall, even the earth with its compulsion to take unto itself all that falls

must know that falling is absurd, yet the girl falling isn't myself,

or she is myself, but a self I took of my own volition unto myself.

Forever. With grace. *This happened.*

Self-Portrait with
Rembrandt Self-Portrait

I put my face inches from his
and look into his eyes
which look back,
but whatever it is
so much beyond suffering
I long towards in his gaze
and imagine inhabiting mine
eludes me.

I put my face inches from his
face palette-knifed nearly raw,
scraped down to whatever it is
that denies flesh yet is flesh
but whatever it is
which still so exalts flesh,
even flesh scraped nearly raw,
eludes me.

My face inches from his
face neither frowning
nor smiling nor susceptible
any longer to any expression
but this watch, this regard;
whatever it is
I might keep of any of that
eludes me.

My face inches from his,
his inches from mine,
whatever it is beyond
dying and fear of dying,
whatever it is beyond solace
which remains solace
eludes me,
yet no longer eludes me.

Oh

Oh my, Harold Brodkey, of all people, after all this time appearing to me,
so long after his death, so even longer since our friendship, our last friendship,
the third or fourth, the one anyway when the ties between us definitively frayed
(Oh, Harold's a handful, another of his ex-friends sympathized, to my relief);

Harold Brodkey, at a Christmas Eve dinner, of all times and places,
because of my nephew's broken nose, of all reasons, which he suffered in an assault,
the bone shattered, reassembled, but healing a bit out of plumb,
and when I saw him something Harold wrote came to mind, about Marlon Brando,

how until Brando's nose was broken he'd been pretty, but after he was beautiful,
and that's the case here, a sensitive boy now a complicatedly handsome young man
with a sinewy edge he hadn't had, which I surely remark because of Harold,
and if I spoke to the dead, which I don't, or not often, I might thank him:

It's pleasant to think of you, Harold, of our good letters and talks;
I'm sorry we didn't make it up that last time, I wanted to but I was worn out
by your snits and rages, your mania to be unlike and greater than anyone else,
your preemptive attacks for inadequate acknowledgment of your genius . . .

But no, leave it alone, Harold's gone, truly gone, and isn't it unforgivable, vile,
to stop loving someone, or to stop being loved; we don't mean to lose friends,
but someone drifts off, and we let them, or they renounce us, or we them, or we're hurt,
like flowers, for god's sake, when really we're prideful brutes, as blunt as icebergs.

Until something like this, some Harold Brodkey wandering into your mind,
as exasperating as ever, and, oh my, as brilliant, as charming, unwound from his web
to confront you with how ridden you are with unthought regret, how diminished,
how well you know you'll clunk on to the next rationalization, the next loss, the next lie.

Dissections

Not only have the skin and flesh and parts of the skeleton
of one of the anatomical effigies in the *Musée de l'Homme*
been excised, stripped away, so that you don't look just at,
but through the thing—pink lungs, red kidney and heart,
tangles of yellowish nerves he seems snarled in, like a net;

not only are his eyes without eyelids, and so shallowly
embedded beneath the blade of the brow, that they seem,
with no shadow to modulate them, flung open in pain or fear;
and not only is his gaze so frenziedly focused that he seems to be
receiving everything, even our regard scraping across him as *blare*;

not only that, but looking more closely, I saw he was real,
that he'd been constructed, reconstructed, on an actual skeleton:
the nerves and organs were wire and plaster, but the armature,
the staring skull, the spine and ribs, were varnished, oxidizing bone;
someone was there, his personhood discernible, a self, a soul.

I felt embarrassed, as though I'd intruded on someone's loneliness,
or grief, and then, I don't know why, it came to me to pray,
though I don't pray, I've unlearned how, to whom, or what,
what fiction, what illusion, or, it wouldn't matter, what true thing,
as mostly I've forgotten how to weep . . . Only mostly, though,

sometimes I can sense the tears in there, and sometimes, yes,
they flow, though rarely for a reason I'd have thought—
a cello's voice will catch in mine, a swerve in a poem, and once,
a death, someone I hardly knew, but I found myself sobbing, sobbing,
for everyone I had known who'd died, and some who almost had.

In the next display hall, evolution: half, then quarter creatures,
Australopithecus, *Pithecanthropus*, *Cro-Magnon*,
sidle diffidently along their rocky winding path towards us.
Flint and fire, science and song, and all of it coming to this,
this unhealable self in myself who knows what I should know.

Inculcations

Only heartbreaking was it much later to first hear someone you loved speak of strangers with
   disdain.
They, them, those: this accent, that hue, these with their filth and squalor, those in their shacks,
   their slums.

We were intelligent, ambitious, appropriately acquisitive; they untrustworthy, ignorant, feckless;
worse, they were presumed to need *less than we, and therefore merited yet more scorn and*
   contempt.

Only saddening a lifetime after to recall those cosmologies of otherness settling comfortably
   within you;
you knew from the tone of their formulation they were despicable, base, but, already tamed,
   you stayed still.

Whence dullness, whence numbness, for so much had to be repudiated or twisted that the senses
   became stone;
whence distrust, and anxiety, for isn't their origin just there, in the impotence and contradiction
   it all implied?

Only appalling now to comprehend that reality could be constructed of expediency, falsehood,
   self-lies;
only worth lamenting now when at last you might but hopelessly won't, for so much else de-
   mands rectification.

Even our notions of beauty, even our modes of adornment; whence suspicion of one's own sensual
   yearnings,
whence dejection, whence rage, all with such labor to be surmounted, while love waited, life
   waited; whence woe.

Whence woe, and the voice far distant within crying out still of what was lost or despoiled. And the cellular flares incessantly flashing, evil and good, yes, no; whence desolation, what never would be.

Sully: Sixteen Months

One more thing to keep:
my second grandson, just
pre-speech, tripping on a toy,
skidding, bump and yowl,

and tears, real tears,
coursing down his cheeks,
until Jessie, cooing, lifts
and holds him to her,

so it's over, but as
they're leaving for home,
he and I alone a moment
in the room where he fell,

he flops down again,
to show me, look,
how it came to pass,
this terrible thing, trilling

syllables for me, no
words yet, but notes,
with hurt in them, and cries,
and that greater cry

that lurks just behind:
right here, he's saying,
on this spot precisely,
here it happened, and yes,

I answer, yes, and so
have the chance to lift him,
too, to hold him, light
and lithe, against me, too.

The World

Splendid that I'd revel even more in the butterflies harvesting pollen
from the lavender in my father-in-law's garden in Normandy
when I bring to mind Francis Ponge's poem where he transfigures them
to levitating matches, and the flowers they dip into to unwashed cups;
it doesn't work with lavender, but still, so lovely, matches, cups,
and lovely, too, to be here in the fragrant summer sunlight reading.

Just now an essay in *Le Monde*, on Fragonard, his oval oil sketch
of a mother opening the bodice of her rosily blushing daughter
to demonstrate to a young artist that the girl would be suitable as a "model";
the snide quotation marks insinuate she might be other than she seems,
but to me she seems entirely enchanting, even without her top
and with the painter's cane casually lifting her skirt from her ankle.

Fragonard needs so little for his plot; the girl's disarranged underslips
a few quick swirls, the mother's compliant mouth a blur, her eyes
two dots of black, yet you can see how crucial this transaction is to her,
how accommodating she'd be in working through potential complications.
In the shadows behind, a smear of fabric spills from a drawer,
a symbol surely, though when one starts thinking symbol, what isn't?

Each sprig of lavender lifting jauntily as its sated butterfly departs,
Catherine beneath the beech tree with her father and sisters, me watching,
everything and everyone might stand for something else, *be* something else.
Though in truth I can't imagine what; reality has put itself so solidly before me
there's little need for mystery . . . Except for us, for how we take the world
to us, and make it more, more than we are, more even than itself.

Of Childhood the Dark

HERE

Uncanny to realize one was *here*, so much
came before the awareness of being here.

Then to suspect your place here was yours only
because no one else wanted or would have it.

A site, a setting, and you the matter to fill it,
though you guessed it could never be filled.

Therefore, as much as a presence, you were a problem,
a task; insoluble, so optional, so illicit.

Then the first understanding: that you
yourself were the difficult thing to be done.

OUTSETS

Even then, though surely I was a "child,"
which implied sense and intent, but no power,

I wasn't what I'd learned a child should be:
I was never naïve, never without guile.

Hardly begun, I was no longer new,
already beset with quandaries and cries.

Was I a molten to harden and anneal, the core
of what I was destined to become, or was I

what I seemed, inconsequential, but free?
But if free, why quandaries, why cries?

DANGER

Watch out, you might fall, as that one fell,
or fall *ill*, as he or she did, or die,

or worse, not die, be insufficient,
less than what should be your worth.

Be cautious of your body, which isn't you,
though neither are you its precise other;

you're what it feels, and the knowing
what's felt, yet no longer quite either.

Your life is first of all what may be lost,
its ultimate end to not end.

AND FEAR

Not lurk, not rancor, not rage, nor,
please, trapping and tearing, yet they were *there*,

from the start, impalpable but prodigious,
ever implicit. Even before anything happens

(how know that this is what happens?),
there was the terror, the wrench and flex,

the being devoured, ingested by terror,
and the hideous inference, that from now

every absence of light would be terror,
every unheard whisper more terror.

THE LESSON

One must be *right*, one's truths must
be *true*, most importantly they,

and you, must be irrefutable, otherwise
they'll lead to humiliation and sin.

Your truths will seek you, though you still
must construct and comprehend them,

then unflinchingly give yourself to them.
More than you, implying more even

than themselves, they are the single matter
for which you must be ready to lie.

THE BAN

Always my awful eyes, and always
the alluring forbidden, always what I'd see

and the delirious behind or beneath; always
taboo twinned with intrigue, prohibition,

and the secret slits, which my gaze, with my assent
or without it, would slip skittering through.

Though nothing was ever as enchanting
as the anticipation of it, always my eyes

would be seeking again all they imagined,
lewd and low, might be hidden from them.

PANDORA

It was clear, now that the story I'd waited
so long for had finally found me,

it was I who englobed the secrets, and the evil,
and the ruined splendor before evil,

for I guessed I'd once been in splendor.
Terrible to have coffered in myself these forebodings,

these atrocious closeds which must never
be opened, but are, ever will be.

Revealed now, though, ratified and released,
at least they were no longer just mine.

GAMES

The others play at violence, then so do I,
though I'd never have imagined

I'd enact this thing of attack,
of betraying, besting, rearing above,

of hand become fist, become bludgeon,
these similes of cruelty, conquest, extinction.

They, we, play at doing away with,
but also at being annulled, falling dead,

as though it were our choice, this learning
to be done away with, to fall dead.

DEVOUT

I knew this couldn't be me, knew this holy
double of me would be taken from me,

would go out to the ravenous rocks to be dust
beneath rock, glint ashudder in dust,

but I knew I'd miss him, my swimmer in the vast;
without him was only mind-gristle and void.

Disbelief didn't drive him from me, nor the thrash
of austerities I gave him to think might be prayer.

Scorn, rather, for me, for my needing reasons to pray,
for the selves I tried to pray into being to pray.

SELF-LOVE

No sooner had I heard of it than I knew
I was despicably, inextricably guilty of it.

It wasn't as I'd hoped that kingdom I'd found
in myself where you whispered to yourself

and heard whispers back: that was iniquity, too,
but was nothing to this; from this, I could tell,

my inept repentances would never redeem me,
so I must never trust myself again,

not the artifice I showed others, still less
that seething, sinful boil within.

FIRST LOVE LOST

The gash I inflict on myself in a sludge-slow
brook in a dip in field of hornets and thorns,

I hardly remark, nor the blood spooled out behind
like a carnivore's track; it brings satisfaction,

as though I'd been tested, and prevailed. And the talon
of pain in my palm? I already know pain,

love's pain, which I know is all pain, just as I know
the river will dry, my filthy wound heal

and the wolf be driven to earth, before love,
love everlasting, will relent or release me.

SENSITIVE

Sensitive on a hillside, sensitive in a dusk,
summer dusk of mown clover exhaling

its opulent languor; sensitive in a gush
of ambient intimation, then inspiration, these forms

not forms bewilderingly weaving towards,
then through me, calling me forth from myself,

from the imperatives which already so drove me:
fused to sense and sensation, to a logic

other than attainment's, unknowns beckoned,
from beyond even the clover and dusk.

MY SADNESS

Not grounded in suffering, nor even
in death, mine or anyone else's,

it was sufficient unto itself, death and pain
were only portions of its inescapable sway.

Nor in being alone, though loneliness contained
much of the world, and infected the rest.

Sadness was the rest; engrossed in it, rapt,
I thought it must be what was called soul.

Don't souls, rapt in themselves, ravish themselves?
Wasn't I rapt? Wasn't I ravaged?

TENSES

Then seemingly all at once there was a *past*,
of which you were more than incidentally composed.

Opaque, dense, delectable as oil paint,
fauceted from a source it itself generated in you,

you were magnified by it, but it could intrude,
and weigh, like an unfathomable obligation.

Everything ending waited there, which meant
much would never be done with, even yourself,

the memory of the thought of yourself you were now,
that thought seemingly always hardly begun.

War

SEPTEMBER—OCTOBER 2001

1.

I keep rereading an article I found recently about how Mayan scribes,
who also were historians, polemicists, and probably poets as well,
when their side lost a war, not a rare occurrence apparently,

there having been a number of belligerent kingdoms
constantly struggling for supremacy, would be disgraced and tortured,
their fingers broken and the nails torn out, and then be sacrificed.

Poor things—the reproduction from a mural shows three:
one sprawls in slack despair, gingerly cradling his left hand with his right,
another gazes at his injuries with furious incomprehension,

while the last lifts his mutilated fingers to the conquering warriors
as though to elicit compassion for what's been done to him: they,
elaborately armored, glowering at one another, don't bother to look.

2.

Like bomber pilots in our day, one might think, with their radar
and their infallible infrared, who soar, unheard, unseen, over generalized,
digital targets that mystically ignite, billowing out from vaporized cores.

Or like the Greek and Trojan gods, when they'd tire of their creatures,
"flesh ripped by the ruthless bronze," and wander off, or like the god
we think of as ours, who found mouths to speak for him, then left.

They fought until nothing remained but rock and dust and shattered bone,
Troy's walls a waste, the stupendous Mesoamerican cities abandoned
to devouring jungle, tumbling on themselves like children's blocks.

And we, alone again under an oblivious sky, were quick to learn
how our best construals of divinity, our *Do unto, Love, Don't kill,*
could be easily garbled to canticles of vengeance and battle prayers.

3·

Fall's first freshness, strange; the seasons' ceaseless wheel,
starlings starting south, the annealed leaves ready to release,
yet still those columns of nothingness rise from their own ruins,

their twisted carcasses of steel and ash still fume, and still,
one by one, tacked up by hopeful lovers, husbands, wives,
the absent faces wait, already tattering, fading, going out.

These things that happen in the particle of time we have to be alive,
these violations which almost more than any ark or altar
embody sanctity by enacting so precisely sanctity's desecration.

These broken voices of bereavement asking of us what isn't to be given.
These suddenly smudged images of consonance and peace.
These fearful burdens to be borne, complicity, contrition, grief.

Fear

SEPTEMBER 2001–AUGUST 2002

1.

At almost the very moment an exterminator's panel truck,
the blowup of a cockroach airbrushed on its side,
pulls up at a house across from our neighborhood park,
a battalion of transient grackles invades the picnic ground,

and the odd thought comes to me how much in their rich sheen,
their sheer abundance, their hunger without end, if I let them
they can seem akin to roaches; even their curt, coarse cry:
mightn't those subversive voices beneath us sound like that?

Roaches, though . . . Last year, our apartment house was overrun,
insecticides didn't work, there'd be roaches on our toothbrushes and combs.
The widower downstairs—this is awful—who'd gone through deportation
and the camps and was close to dying now and would sometimes faint,

was found one morning lying wedged between his toilet and a wall,
naked, barely breathing, the entire surface of his skin alive
with the insolent, impervious brutes, who were no longer daunted
by the light, or us—our Samaritan neighbor had to scrape them off.

2.

Vermin, poison, atrocious death: what different resonance they have
in our age of suicide as armament, anthrax, resurrected pox.
Every other week brings new warnings, new false alarms;
it's hard to know how much to be afraid, or even how.

Once I knew, too well; I was of the generation of the bomb—
Hiroshima, the broiling bubble at Bikini, ICBMs.
The Second World War was barely over, in annihilated cities
children just my age still foraged for scraps of bread,

and we were being taught that our war would be nuclear,
that if we weren't incinerated, the flesh would rot from our bones.
By the time Kennedy and Khrushchev faced off over Cuba,
rockets primed and aimed, we were sick with it, insane.

And now these bewildering times, when those whose interest is
to consternate us hardly bother to conceal their purposes.
Yes, we have antagonists, and some of their grievances are just,
but is no one blameless, are we all to be combatants, prey?

3.

We have offended very grievously, and been most tyrannous,
wrote Coleridge, invasion imminent from radical France;
the wretched plead against us . . . Then, *Father and God,*
spare us, he begged, as I suppose one day I will as well.

I still want to believe we'll cure the human heart, heal it
of its anxieties, and the mistrust and barbarousness they spawn,
but hasn't that metaphorical heart been slashed, dissected,
cauterized and slashed again, and has the carnage relented, ever?

Night nearly, the exterminator's gone, the park deserted,
the swings and slides my grandsons play on forsaken.
In the windows all around, the flicker of the television news:
more politics of terror; war, threats of war, war without end.

A half-chorus of grackles still ransacks the trash;
in their intricate iridescence they seem eerily otherworldly,
negative celestials, risen from some counter-realm to rescue us.
But now, scattering towards the deepening shadows, they go, too.

Chaos

I saw a spider on a library cornice snatch a plump,
brightly lacquered as-a-yellow-pepper beetle
and dash—that was the word—across its system of webs
until it came to a dark lair where it let itself fall,
settle, and avidly, methodically, with evident delectation,
devour its still so sadly brilliantly hued prey.

All this took place in a dream, but even when I woke,
my revulsion wouldn't abate, nor my dread,
because when I followed the associative tracks
that had brought me to engender such harshness in myself,
I kept being driven further than I wanted to go,
arriving at conclusions I'd never usually entertain.

The beetle, I thought, was the generalized human person,
gullible, malleable, impotent, self-destructive—
gullible, above all, is what kept coming to me;
how the prospect of living without anxiety renders us
ever more anxious, more ready to accede
to interests which clearly contradict ours.

The spider was power, plus limitless greed,
plus an abstraction, not God, but something like God,
which perpetrates something like Babel on us,
within us, though, in our genes; that twist of something
which keeps us with only this many words, and no more,
leaving us all but incoherent to ourselves, thus easily misled.

But why, even in dreams, must I dwell on the dark,
the dire, the *dreck*? A foal in a dappling field,
I might have dreamed, a child trailing after with a rope,
but no, the sense, the scent nearly, the dream-scent,
was wild frustration; not pity but some insane collision
with greed, and power, and credulity, above all.

Perhaps I slept then, perhaps I dreamed my muse,
to whom when she appears I too often say,
"You're not as seemly as I believed, nor as pure,"
and my muse forsakes me. But perhaps the spider is muse,
or the beetle, or Babel; no wonder she'd betray me,
no wonder, bending her languorous note, she'd forsake me.

The Hearth

FEBRUARY 2003

1.

Alone after the news on a bitter
evening in the country, sleet slashing
the stubbled fields, the river ice;
I keep stirring up the recalcitrant fire,

but when I throw my plastic coffee cup
in with new kindling it perches intact
on a log for a strangely long time,
as though uncertain what to do,

until, in a somehow reluctant, almost
creaturely way, it dents, collapses,
and decomposes to a dark slime
untwining itself on the stone hearth.

I once knew someone who was caught in a fire
and made it sound something like that.
He'd been loading a bomber and a napalm shell
had gone off; flung from the flames,

at first he felt nothing and thought
he'd been spared, but then came the pain,
then the hideous dark—he'd been blinded,
and so badly charred he spent years

in recovery: agonizing debridements,
grafts, learning to speak through a mouth
without lips, to read Braille with fingers
lavaed with scar, to not want to die—

though that never happened. He swore,
even years later, with a family,
that if he were back there, this time allowed
to put himself out of his misery, he would.

2.

There was dying here tonight, after
dusk, by the road: an owl,
eyes fixed and flared, breast
so winter-white he seemed to shine

a searchlight on himself, helicoptered
near a wire fence, then suddenly
banked, plunged, and vanished
into the swallowing dark with his prey.

Such an uncomplicated departure;
no detonation, nothing to mourn;
if the creature being torn from its life
made a sound, I didn't hear it.

But in fact I wasn't listening, I was thinking,
as I often do these days, of war;
I was thinking of my children, and their children,
of the more than fear I feel for them,

and then of radar, rockets, shrapnel,
cities razed, soil poisoned
for a thousand generations; of suffering so vast
it nullifies everything else.

I stood in the wind in the raw cold
wondering how those with power over us
can effect such things, and by what
cynical reasoning pardon themselves.

The fire's ablaze now, its glow
on the windows makes the night even darker,
but it barely keeps the room warm.
I stoke it again, and crouch closer.

Low Relief

They hunted lions, they hunted humans, and enslaved them.
One lion, I recall, had been viciously speared; he vomited blood,
his hindquarters dragged behind him like cement in a sack.

Spirits with wings and the heads of eagles flanked them;
the largest sports a rosette on a band on his wrist, like a watch:
a wristwatch measuring blossomings, measuring lives.

They wore skirts, helmets, their beards were permanent-waved.
Carved in stone, enameled in brick, in chariots, on thrones,
always that resolute, unblinking profile of composure.

Did they as they hunted feel sure of themselves,
did they believe they enacted what their cosmos demanded?
Did a god ring through them like a phone going off on a bus?

On each block, each slab, each surface, a slave,
each bound with a cable of what must feel like steel;
their heads loll: hear them cry pitiably into the stone.

Did they have gods who were evil others, like ours?
Even colder than they, indifferent, more given to fury,
vindictive, venomous, stutteringly stupid, like ours?

Their forearms were striated like Blake's ghost of a flea's,
they never savaged themselves in their souls, though;
how lightly they bear the weight of their extinction.

Coherence, things in proper relation, did it fail them?
Was unreason all around, and confusion and depression,
and no coherent, convincing model to explain why?

They move left to right, right to left, like lanes of traffic.
They, too, perhaps, found no place to stand still, to judge,
to believe wickedness will never be forgotten nor forgiven.

Also gazelles, beasts of the air, and eyes which contain,
and ears which submit; dew of morn, blaze of noon,
the faces before you wild with the erotics of existence.

And that coming someday to know how foolish,
even confronting the end of one's world, to think
one might spare oneself by doing away with oneself.

Their palace doors were cedar strapped with stout bronze.
The lions, inexhaustibly fierce, never retreat, never give in.
One, off near a column of slaves, glares back at us as she dies.

The Tract

1.

Where is it where is it where is it in what volume what text what treatise what tract
is that legend that tale that myth homily parable fable that's haunted me since I read it
I thought in Campbell but I can't find it or some scripture some Veda not there either
that holy history anyway from those years when I was trying to skull a way out of the flat
banal world which so oppressed me I'm sure because it contained me wherever it came from
it's haunted me haunted me lurking in everything I've thought or felt or had happen to me

2.

The protagonist's not anyone special just a man he's born grows marries has children
he's living his life like everyone else pleasure pain pleasure pain then one day a flood
a deluge roars through his valley sweeping all before it away his house his village the people
only he and his family are left clinging to a tree then his wife's torn from his arms
then his children too one by one then the tree is uprooted and he himself is boiled out
into the wild insatiable waves he cries out for his life goes under comes up sinks again

3.

and rises to the surface to find himself on an ocean a vast sea and looming far above him
is a god a god sleeping it's Vishnu if I remember Vishnu asleep swaying serenely like a lotus
and as the person gazes in awe the god wakes sees the man plucks him from the waves
and thrusts him into his mouth and there in that eternally empty darkness the man realizes
that oh all he'd lived the days hours years the emotions thoughts even his family oh
were illusion reality was this all along this god huge as a storm cloud the horizonless sea

4.

Not only in depression does that tale still come back to attack me not only in melancholy
am I infected by its annihilating predications though I've been gloomy enough often enough
mostly early on about love then the political bedlam then work absurd writing a word
striking it out while all around you as the books of truth say is suffering and suffering
at first it would take me yes during desponds but even at moments of passion when everything
but what you want and the force of your want is obliterated except at mind's reaches

5.

where ancient mills keep heart and brain pumping and some blessed apparatus of emotion
and counter-emotion keeps you from weeping with the desolation that lurks in desire
a desolation I don't thank goodness feel anymore not during passion now does that story
secrete its acids through me but still it does take me I want to say when my vigilance flags
when I don't pay attention then the idea it postulates or the chilling suspicion it confirms
leaves me riven with anxiety for all that exists or has ever existed or seemed to

6.

Yet what is there in that no way plausible whatever it is that can still so afflict me
philosophically primitive spiritually having nothing to do with any tradition even the tragic
to which I feel linked if the wisdom it's meant to impart is that you can't countervail misery
with gratification or that to imagine life without suffering is to suffer I've learned that
and it doesn't make death more daunting I have death more or less in its place now
though the thought still sears of a consciousness not even one's own extinguished

7.

Not some rage of mentalism then something simpler though more frightening about love
that the man has negated in him not only the world but his most precious sentiments
what's dire is that the story denies and so promulgates the notion that one can deny
the belief no the conviction that some experiences love most of all can must be exempted
from even the most cruelly persuasive skepticism and excluded even from implications
of one's own cosmology if they too radically rupture what links real lives one to another

8.

To release yourself from attachment so from despair I suppose was the point of the text
and I suppose I was looking for it again to release me from *it* and if I haven't done that
at least I'm somewhere near the opposite where I'm hanging on not to a tree in a dream
but to the hope that someday I'll accept without qualm or question that the reality of others
the love of others the miracle of others all that which feels like enough is truly enough
no celestial sea no god in his barque of being just life just hanging on for dear life

From

Wait

(2010)

The Gaffe

1.

If that someone who's me yet not me yet who judges me is always with me,
as he is, shouldn't he have been there when I said so long ago that thing I said?

If he who rakes me with such not trivial shame for minor sins now were there then,
shouldn't he have warned me he'd even now devastate me for my unpardonable affront?

I'm a child then, yet already I've composed this conscience-beast, who harries me:
is there anything else I can say with certainty about who I was, except that I, that he,

could already draw from infinitesimal transgressions complex chords of remorse,
and orchestrate ever-undiminishing retribution from the hapless rest of myself?

2.

The son of some friends of my parents has died, and my parents, paying their call,
take me along, and I'm sent out with the dead boy's brother and some others to play.

We're joking around, and words come to my mind, which to my amazement are said.
How do you know when you can laugh when somebody dies, your brother dies?

is what's said, and the others go quiet, the backyard goes quiet, everyone stares,
and I want to know now why that someone in me who's me yet not me let me say it.

Shouldn't he have told me the contrition cycle would from then be ever upon me,
it didn't matter that I'd really only wanted to know how grief ends, and when?

3.

I could hear the boy's mother sobbing inside, then stopping, sobbing then stopping.
Was the end of her grief already there? Had her someone in her told her it would end?

Was her someone in her kinder to her, not tearing at her, as mine did, still does, me,
for guessing grief someday ends? Is that why her sobbing stopped sometimes?

She didn't laugh, though, or I never heard her. *How do you know when you can laugh?*
Why couldn't someone have been there in me not just to accuse me, but to explain?

The kids were playing again, I was playing, I didn't hear anything more from inside.
The way now sometimes what's in me is silent, too, and sometimes, though never really, forgets.

Marina

As I'm reading Tsvetaeva's essays,
Art in the Light of Conscience,
stunning—*"Art, a series of answers*
to which there are no questions"—
a tiny insect I don't recognize
is making its way across my table.
It has lovely transparent wings
but for some reason they drag behind
as it treks the expanse of formica
and descends into a crack.

"To each answer before it evaporates,
our *question"*: composed in Paris
during the difficult years of exile.
But which of her years were easy?
This at least was before the husband,
a spy, an assassin, went back,
then she, too, with her son,
to the Soviet madhouse, back . . .
"This being outgalloped by answers,
is inspiration . . ." Outgalloped!

Still lugging its filigreed train,
the insect emerges: fragile, distracted,
it can't even trace a straight line,
but it circumnavigates the table.
Does it know it's back where it began?

Still, it perseveres, pushing
courageously on, one inch, another . . .
"Art . . . a kind of physical world
of the spiritual . . . A spiritual world
of the physical . . . almost flesh."

One daughter, dying, at three,
of hunger, the other daughter,
that gift of a sugar cube,
in her mouth, drenched with blood . . .
"A poet is an answer . . . not to the blow,
but a quivering of the air."
The years of wandering,
the weary return, husband betrayed,
arrested, daughter in a camp . . .
"The soul is our capacity for pain."

When I breathe across it,
the bug squats, quakes, finally flies.
And couldn't she have fled again,
again have been flown? Couldn't she,
noose in her hand, have proclaimed,
"I am Tsvetaeva," and then not?
No, no time now for "then not . . ."
But *"Above poet, more than poet . . ."*
she'd already said it, already sung it:
"Air finished. Firmament now."

On the Métro

On the métro, I have to ask a young woman to move the packages beside her to make room
   for me;
she's reading, her foot propped on the seat in front of her, and barely looks up as she pulls
   them to her.
I sit, take out my own book—Cioran, *The Temptation to Exist*—and notice her glancing up
   from hers
to take in the title of mine, and then, as Gombrowicz puts it, she "affirms herself physically,"
   that is,
becomes *present* in a way she hadn't been before: though she hasn't moved, she's allowed
   herself
to come more sharply into focus, be more accessible to my sensual perception, so I can't help
   but remark
her strong figure and very tan skin—(how literally golden young women can look at the end
   of summer).
She leans back now, and as the train rocks and her arm brushes mine she doesn't pull it away;
she seems to be allowing our surfaces to unite: the fine hairs on both our forearms, sensitive,
   alive,
achingly alive, bring news of someone touched, someone sensed, and thus acknowledged,
   known.

I understand that in no way is she offering more than this, and in truth I have no desire for
   more,
but it's still enough for me to be taken by a surge, first of warmth then of something like its
   opposite:
a memory—a girl I'd mooned for from afar, across the table from me in the library in school
   now,

our feet I thought touching, touching even again, and then, with all I craved that touch to mean,

my having to realize it wasn't her flesh my flesh for that gleaming time had pressed, but the table leg.

The young woman today removes her arm now, stands, swaying against the lurch of the slowing train,

and crossing before me brushes my knee and does that thing again, asserts her bodily being again

(Gombrowicz again), then quickly moves to the door of the car and descends, not once looking back

(to my relief not looking back), and I allow myself the thought that though I'm probably to her again

as senseless as that table of my youth, as wooden, as unfeeling, perhaps there was a moment I was not.

We

A basset hound with balls
so heavy they hang
a harrowing half
inch from the pavement,

ears cocked, accusingly
watches as his beautiful
mistress croons
to her silver cell phone.

She does, yes, go on,
but my, so slim-
waistedly
does she sway there,

so engrossedly does her dark
gaze drift
towards even
for a moment mine . . .

Though Mister Dog of course
sits down right
then to lick
himself, his groin of course,

till she cuts off, and he,
gathering his folds
and flab, heaves
erect to leave with her . . .

But wait, she's turning to
a great Ducati
cycle gleaming
black and chromy at the curb,

she's mounting it (that long
strong lift of flank!),
snorting it to life,
coaxing it in gear . . .

Why, she's not his at all!
No more than mine!
What was he thinking?
What was I? Like a wing,

a wave, she banks away
now, downshifts,
pops and crackles
round the curve, is gone.

How sleek she was, though,
how scrufty, how
anciently scabby
we, he and I;

how worn, how
self-devoured,
balls and all,
balls, balls and all.

Saddening

Saddening, worse, to read in "Frost at Midnight,"
Coleridge's ecstatic hymn to his newborn son Hartley,
for whom he imagines ". . . all seasons shall be sweet,"
and to find in the biographies how depressingly
their relationship deteriorated when the boy was grown:
the father struggling between his dependence on opiates
and the exertions of his recalcitrant genius, the son trying
to separate from the mostly absent but still intimidating father.

Their final contact has Hartley, a neophyte poet himself—
he'll never attain stature—abandoning his father in the street,
Coleridge in tears, not knowing, as though he were a character
in one of the more than minor tragedies he might have written
if his life had evolved more fortuitously, how to begin
to reconcile his unspoken suffering with his son's,
how to conceive of healing the hurt both had to have felt
before each reeled back to his respective isolation.

The myth was already in effect then—Wordsworth's doing?—
that creativity like Coleridge's thrives best in seclusion.
Even Coleridge, though his poem takes place with his son
beside him and friends sleeping yards away, speaks of
". . . that solitude, which suits abstruser musings . . ."
So generations of writers go off to the woods, to find . . .
alcohol—Schwartz, Lowry, too many others to mention—
depression or even—Lowell, one hates to say it—wife abuse.

Coleridge in fact was rarely out of some intimate situation
for five minutes in his life, sharing his friend's houses
and tables, and there's the scene, saddening, too, worse,
of the poet imploring the captain of the ship ferrying him
home from Malta to administer an enema to unclog
the impacted feces of his laudanum-induced constipation.
Daily stuff for Coleridge—he hardly remarks it, poor man, poor giant—
excruciating for us, spoiled as we are, sanitized, tamed . . .

But what does the life—dope, shit, neurosis, fathers or sons—
have to do with anything anyway? Think of innocent Clare,
twenty-eight years in the madhouse, and isn't there some *fairness*,
you might think, some *justice*, but letting yourself think that,
there's nowhere to go but bitterness, and how regret
that deluge of masterpieces to rejoice in? Coleridge, anyway,
at the end found fulfillment, and Clare, too, if not fulfillment,
then something, perhaps acceptance; even Hartley, too, something.

I was there once, in that cottage, a packet of ill-lit rooms,
at the very spot, beside the hearth, where the poem was made—
(". . . the thin blue flame . . . that film which fluttered on the grate . . .").
You could still sense something in that comfortless cell
resonating with youth and hope, which, almost on his deathbed,
Coleridge wrote, ". . . *embracing, seen as one, were love.*"
Outside, the luminous sea, the hills: easy to understand hoping
to stay in such a world forever, and the qualm to tear yourself away.

Shrapnel

1.

Seven hundred tons per inch, I read, is the force in a bomb or shell in the microsecond after
   its detonation,

and two thousand feet per second is the speed at which the shrapnel, the materials with which
   the ordnance

is packed, plus its burst steel casing, "stretched, thinned, and sharpened" by the tremendous
   heat and energy,

are propelled outwards in an arc until they strike an object and either ricochet or become em-
   bedded in it.

In the case of insufficiently resistant materials, the shards of shrapnel can cause "significant
   damage";

in human tissue, for instance, rupturing flesh and blood vessels and shattering and splintering
   bone.

Should no essential organs be involved, the trauma may be termed "superficial," as by the
   chief nurse,

a nun, in Ian McEwan's *Atonement*, part of which takes place in a hospital receiving wounded
   from Dunkirk.

It's what she says when a soldier cries, *"Fuck!"* as her apprentice, the heroine, a young writer-
   to-be,

probes a wound with her forceps to extract one of many jagged fragments of metal from a sol-
   dier's legs.

"Fuck!" was not to be countenanced back then. "How dare you speak that way?" scolds the
   imperious sister,

"your injuries are superficial, so consider yourself lucky and show some courage worthy of
   your uniform."

The man stays still after that, though "he sweated and . . . his knuckles turned white round
the iron bedhead."
"Only seven to go," the inexperienced nurse chirps, but the largest chunk, which she's saved
for last, resists;
at one point it catches, protruding from the flesh—("He bucked on the bed and hissed through
his teeth")—
and not until her third resolute tug does the whole "gory, four-inch stiletto of irregular steel"
come clear.

   2.

"Shrapnel throughout the body" is how a ten-year-old killed in a recent artillery offensive is
described.
"Shrapnel throughout the body": the phrase is repeated along with the name of each deceased
child
in the bulletin released as propaganda by our adversaries, at whose operatives the barrage
was directed.
There are photos as well—one shows a father rushing through the street, his face torn with a
last frantic hope,

his son in his arms, rag-limp, chest and abdomen speckled with deep, dark gashes and smears
of blood.
Propaganda's function, of course, is exaggeration: the facts are there, though, the child is there
. . . or not there.
. . . As the shrapnel is no longer there in the leg of the soldier: the girl holds it up for him to
see, the man quips,
"Run him under the tap, Nurse, I'll take him home," then, ". . . he turned to the pillow and be-
gan to sob."

Technically, I read, what's been called shrapnel here would have once been defined as "splinters" or "fragments."

"Shrapnel" referred then only to a spherical shell, named after its inventor, Lieutenant Henry Shrapnel.

First used in 1804, it was ". . . guaranteed to cause heavy casualties . . . the best mankiller the army possessed."

Shrapnel was later awarded a generous stipend in recognition of his contribution "to the state of the art."

Where was I? The nun, the nurse; the nurse leaves the room, throws up; the fictional soldier, the real child . . .

The father . . . What becomes of the father? He skids from the screen, from the page, from the mind . . .

Shrapnel's device was superseded by higher-powered, more efficient projectiles, obsolete now in their turn.

One war passes into the next. One wound is the next and the next. Something howls. Something cries.

Wood

That girl I didn't love, then because she was going to leave me, loved,
that girl, that Sunday when I stopped by and she was in bed in her nightgown
(it only came to me later that someone else had just, good god, been with her),

that girl, when my hand touched her belly, under her plush mesh nightgown,
began turning her belly to wood—I hadn't known this could be done,
that girls, that humans, could do this—then, when all her belly was wood,

she began turning the rest of herself to perhaps something harder, steel,
or harder; perhaps she was turning herself, her entire, once so soft self,
to some unknown mineral substance found only on other, very far planets,

planets with chemical storms and vast, cold ammonia oceans of ice,
and I just had to pretend—I wasn't taking this lightly, I wasn't a kid anymore—
that I wasn't one of those pitted, potato-shaped moons with precarious orbits,

and then I was out, in the street—it was still Sunday, though I don't recall bells—
and she, where did she go, dear figment, dear fragment, where are you now,
in your nightgown, in your bed, steel and wood? Dear steel, dear wood.

Cassandra, Iraq

1.

She's magnificent, as we imagine women must be
who foresee and foretell and are right and disdained.

This is the difference between us who are like her
in having been right and disdained, and us as we are.

Because we, in our foreseeings, our having been right,
are repulsive to ourselves, fat and immobile, like toads.

Not toads in the garden, who after all are what they are,
but toads in the tale of death in the desert of sludge.

2.

In this tale of lies, of treachery, of superfluous dead,
were there ever so many who were right and disdained?

With no notion what to do next? If we were true seers,
as prescient as she, as frenzied, we'd know what to do next.

We'd twitter, as she did, like birds; we'd warble, we'd trill.
But what would it be really, to *twitter*, to *warble*, to *trill*?

Is it *ee-ee-ee*, like having a child? Is it *uh-uh-uh*, like a wound?
Or is it inside, like a blow, silent to everyone but yourself?

3.

Yes, inside, I remember, *oh-oh-oh*: it's where grief
is just about to be spoken, but all at once can't be: *oh*.

When you no longer can "think" of what things like lies,
like superfluous dead, so many, might mean: *oh*.

Cassandra will be abducted at the end of her tale, and die.
Even she can't predict how. Stabbed? Shot? Blown to bits?

Her abductor dies, too, though, in a gush of gore, in a net.
That we know; she foresaw that—in a gush of gore, in a net.

Light

Another drought morning after a too-brief dawn downpour,
uncountable silvery glitterings on the leaves of the withering maples—

I think of a troop of the blissful blessed approaching Dante,
"a hundred spheres shining," he rhapsodizes, "the purest pearls . . . ,"

then of the frightening, brilliant, myriad gleam in my lamp
of the eyes of the vast swarm of bats I found once in a cave,

a chamber whose walls seethed with a spaceless carpet of creatures,
their cacophonous, keen, insistent, incessant squeakings and squealings

churning the warm, rank, cloying air; of how one,
perfectly still among all the fitfully twitching others,

was looking straight at me, gazing solemnly, thoughtfully up
from beneath the intricate furl of its leathery wings

as though it couldn't believe I was there, or was trying to place me,
to situate me in the gnarl we'd evolved from, and now,

the trees still heartrendingly asparkle, Dante again,
this time the way he'll refer to a figure he meets as "the life of . . . ,"

not the soul, or person, the *life*, and once more the bat, and I,
our lives in that moment together, our lives, our *lives*,

his with no vision of celestial splendor, no poem,
mine with no flight, no unblundering dash through the dark,

his without realizing it would, so soon, no longer exist,
mine having to know for us both that everything ends,

world, afterworld, even their memory, steamed away
like the film of uncertain vapor of the last of the luscious rain.

Assumptions

That there is an entity, vast, omnipotent but immaterial, inaccessible to all human sense save
   hearing;
that this entity has a voice with which it can, or at least could once, speak, and in a possibly
   historical
but credible even if mythic past it did speak, to a small group of human beings, always male.

That not only did these primordial addressees receive the entity's disclosures with perfect
   accuracy,
they also transcribed them (writing them down as they were spoken but no matter if years
   later)
literally, with precision, and no patching of gaps with however inspired imaginative spackle.

That the disseminators, adepts, prophets, priests, of these forbiddingly complicated in-
   scribings,
these clumps of bebannered slashes of chisel or quill, interpreted them so as to extract
   correctly
the mostly illogical imperatives, prohibitions, and rigorous modes of existence implied in
   them.

That inherent in these interpretations was the thesis that the now silent entity intended its
   legitimacy
to be transferred to various social institutions, which, though in no obvious relation to it itself,
would have the prerogative to enact in its name anything necessary for the perpetuation of
   their dominion.

That what is often specified by the inheritors of those thrice-removed sanctifications, that cer-
   tain other groups,

by virtue of being in even potential disagreement with the entity's even tacit wishes, become offensive,

and must be amputated, slaughtered, has been deduced correctly from these syllogistic tangles.

That the corollary also holds: that those selected to commit slaughter shall be prepared to *be* slaughtered,

to give up this life, this brilliance—(can't you see how briefly it gleams, this sliver, this glimpse?)—

gamble away, discard, the absolutely precious fragment of time and space they have been granted.

That the "leaders," who orchestrate and finally most benefit from this slaughterer-slaughteree equation,

having slathered themselves with entity-merit, are to be considered uniquely necessary and essential,

and so exempted from any harmful or potentially harmful results of what they themselves effect.

And that all this will continue, go on and on, the same formulations, same unfaltering faulty logic,

same claim of truth extracted from the ticks of good or bad, yes and no, existence, non-existence,

these binomial mental knots we suffer and destroy for, and which go on and on, on and on and on.

All but Always

1.

If you were to possess a complicated
apparatus composed of many
intricate elements and operating
through a number of apparently unpredictable
processes, and if it were asked of you
to specify which parts of this contrivance
you had fabricated and which had come
to you already shaped and assembled,
which of its workings you'd conceived of
and set in motion yourself
and which were already under way
when it came into your possession,

2.

and if you were unable to give
an unqualified response to these questions,
but were forced to admit that you
couldn't say with certainty whether
the activities of the thing were your doing
or the result of some other agency,
or even if its real purposes
had been decided by you, or anyone,
whether there was even a reason

for its being, other than
its always having been,
as far back as you can recall,

3.

and if it came to you that this
mechanism of yours had all
but always run erratically, seemed
all but always in need of repair,
how go about repairing it
if you didn't know whether your notions
of how it worked were grounded
in more than wild surmise, if in fact
you weren't certain what to *call*
the thing—your mind, your self, your life?
What if indeed it was your mind, your self,
your life? What then? What then?

Back

First I did my thing, that's to say her thing, to her, for her,
then she did her thing, I mean my thing, to me, for me,
then we did our thing together, then again, the other way though,
then once more that way again,
then we were done, and we were at dinner,
though I desperately missed the other things now,
and said so:
"Don't you know I can't enjoy anything else now?"
and, still love-tipsy, love-stunned,
"Ever," I said: "I'll never enjoy anything else, ever again."

Except I also meant this,
I mean this being together thinking of that,
or not even her thinking—who knows what she's thinking—
I mean me thinking of that, of her, thinking and thinking,
but now that I've told her, told you, are we then,
back to, again, that?
Yes, and thank goodness I'm back there, we're back there,
I missed you out here by myself, even thinking of that,
which is why I had to do all this thinking,
to take us even in such a partial way back.

Halo

1.

In the desert, a halo around the sun, a vast, prismed disk
with within it another smaller though still huge second circle,
of a slightly darker hue, the furnacing glare precisely in its center.

Suspended above us, so much a different scale from anything here,
it seems not merely light refracted, but some more solid substance;
it *weighs*, and instead of dissipating like an ordinary rainbow,

it stays intact, looms, forebodes, becomes a possible threat,
the outcome of an error, an incipient retaliation, who knows what for?
Perhaps something so dire it shouldn't be thought of.

2.

In a book in the fifties, the then-famous Jesuit scientist
Teilhard de Chardin posited a theory this puts me in mind of:
a bubble around the earth, a "noosphere" he called it,

consisting of all the yearnings, prayers, pleas, entreaties,
of humans for something beyond—he meant god, of course,
Christ—towards which he believed the universe was evolving.

Ingenious: an extra-material layer, numinous, literalized—
he'd even made drawings—very seductive for people like me,
who had no god, no Christ, but thought they might like to.

3.

I still do, sometimes, wish I could believe. More often,
I'd like the whole holiness business gone once and for all,
the reflexive referencing to what I know isn't there,

the craving for retribution for the unjust at the end of the chain.
It's resistant as rock, though, like trying to get shed of the myth
of Adam and Eve, who you know can't be real, to put in their stead

the pair of sooty, stinking, starving Cro-Magnons who are.
Those bedtime stories, those nightmares, feel hammered
like nails into my mind, sometimes it seems they might *be* mind.

4.

Now this, a puncture in the heavens, a rent, a tear,
aglow at the edges but dull within, matte, unreflecting,
a great open thing, like an eye; some sensory Cyclops

perceiving all but attentive to nothing (*blind*, I think, *numb*),
that makes us believe there are matters not to be thought of,
gaps within and between us, fissures, abysses,

that only leaps of forgiveness might span, might heal.
An angel-less halo, the clear gore of light pouring through
without meaning or reason: *blind*, I think, *numb*.

Apes

One branch, I read, of a species of chimpanzees has something like territorial wars,
and when the . . . army, I suppose you'd call it, of one tribe prevails and captures an enemy,
"several males hold a hand or foot of the rival so the victim can be damaged at will."

This is so disquieting: if beings with whom we share so many genes can be this cruel,
what hope for us? Still, "rival," "victim," "will"—don't such anthropomorphic terms
make those simians' social-political conflicts sound more brutal than they are?

The chimps that Catherine and I saw on their island sanctuary in Uganda we loathed.
Unlike the pacific gorillas in the forest of Bwindi, they fought, dementedly shrieked,
the dominant male lorded it over the rest; they were, in all, too much like us.

Another island from my recent reading, where Columbus, on his last voyage,
encountering some "Indians" who'd greeted him with curiosity and warmth, wrote,
before he chained and enslaved them, "They don't even know how to kill each other."

It's occurred to me I've read enough; at my age all I'm doing is confirming my sadness.
Surely the papers: war, terror, torture, corruption—it's like broken glass in the mind.
Back when I knew I knew nothing, I read all the time, poems, novels, philosophy, myth,

but I hardly glanced at the news, there was a distance between what could happen
and the part of myself I felt with: now everything's so tight against me I hardly can move.
The *Analects* say people in the golden age weren't aware they were governed; they just lived.

Could I have passed through my own golden age and not even known I was there?
Some gold: nuclear rockets aimed at your head, racism, sexism, contempt for the poor.
And there I was, reading. What did I learn? Everything, nothing, too little, too much . . .
Just enough to get me here: a long-faced, white-haired ape with a book, still turning the page.

Wait

Chop, hack, slash; chop, hack, slash; cleaver, boning knife, ax—
not even the clumsiest clod of a butcher could do this so crudely,
time, as do you, dismember me, render me, leave me slop in a pail,
one part of my body a hundred years old, one not even there anymore,
another still riven with idiot vigor, voracious as the youth I was
for whom everything always was going too slowly, too slowly.

It was me then who chopped, slashed, through you, across you,
relished you, gorged on you, slugged your invisible liquor down raw.
Now you're polluted; pulse, clock, calendar taint you, befoul you,
you suck at me, pull at me, barbed-wire knots of memory tear me,
my heart hangs, inert, a tag end of tissue, firing, misfiring,
trying to heave itself back to its other way with you.

But was there ever really any other way with you? When I ran
as though for my life, wasn't I fleeing from you, or for you?
Wasn't I frightened you'd fray, leave me nothing but shreds?
Aren't I still? When I snatch at one of your moments, and clutch it,
a pebble, a planet, isn't it wearing away in my hand as though I,
not you, were the ocean of acid, the corrosive in which I dissolve?

Wait, though, wait: I should tell you, too, how happy I am,
how I love it so much, all of it, chopping and slashing and all.
Please know I love especially you, how every morning you turn over
the languorous earth, for how would she know otherwise to do dawn,
to do dusk, when all she hears from her speech-creatures is "Wait!"?
We whose anguished wish is that our last word not be "Wait."

The Coffin Store

I was lugging my death from Kampala to Kraków.
Death, what a ridiculous load you can be,
like the world trembling on Atlas's shoulders.

In Kampala I'd wondered why the people, so poor,
didn't just kill me. *Why don't they kill me?*
In Kraków I must have fancied I'd find poets to talk to.

I still believed then I'd domesticated my death,
that he'd no longer gnaw off my fingers and ears.
We even had parties together: "Happy," said death,

and gave me my present, a coffin, my coffin,
made in Kampala, with a sliding door in its lid,
to look through, at the sky, at the birds, at Kampala.

That was his way, I soon understood, of reverting
to talon and snarl, for the door refused to come open:
no sky, no bird, no poets, no Kraków.

Catherine came to me then, came to me then,
"Open your eyes, mon amour," but death
had undone me, my knuckles were raw as an ape's,

my mind slid like a sad-ankled skate, and no matter
what Catherine was saying, was sighing, was singing,
"Mon amour, mon amour," the door stayed shut, oh, shut.

I heard trees being felled, skinned, smoothed,
hammered together as coffins. I heard death
snorting and stamping, impatient to be hauled off, away.

But here again was Catherine, sighing, and singing,
and the tiny carved wooden door slid ajar, just enough:
the sky, one single bird, Catherine: just enough.

Roe vs. Wade

I wonder if any male but me is still living who remembers
that pre-Roe-Wade abortionist doctor who demanded
along with his payment a kiss, a soul kiss, as it was called then.

And isn't that what it felt like, those astounding first times
her tongue slid warm and wet and alive onto yours,
that something you might call your soul had been revealed?

It was another thing with that backstreet lech, for a woman,
a girl—the one who told me had been barely eighteen;
she shuddered just to remember, in rage, or terror.

I was glad not to have had to have been there.
This was years after; we were in bed, we'd make love;
so lithe she was, with such ardor she worked me in deeper.

I only found out later from friends that after that one
she'd had another adventure, in a hotel in New York:
someone with a coat hanger she'd been told was a "midwife"—

hemorrhage, infection, and she was left sterile.
As many times as we were together, she never told me,
nor told me either that she was on dope, all day every day.

Why she'd trust me with the one story but not the other,
with her body, but not with what she was doing to it . . .
Just more of the miserable mysteries of that time.

Still, Again: Martin Luther King, April 4, 2008

THE RETURN

On something like a plane he returns circling over rows of suburban monopoly houses
in something like a taxi he careens down the garbage-strewn parkways through the slums
of one city the slums of another stores shuttered and locked windows cinder blocked shut
men idling around fires in barrels children foraging dumpsters women asleep in the gutter
drunks beggars pavements littered with bottles vials and syringes then he can't do it anymore
he can't stand anymore what he sees *Not again* he keeps thinking *Not still* and closes his eyes
but that's not enough *Not still* he keeps thinking and forces himself down begins sinking down
instead of arriving he drives himself under the surface *Not still Not again* he rushes along
under the ground hurtling so fast he can't tell where he's going in the darkness under it all
promising himself never again to rise up to the mass of pain there never come to the surface

THE DARKNESS

Yet even there in the dark with him he senses the children the babies the crack babies floating
in their darkness the AIDS babies torn with seizures he feels them with him the lost children
their brain cells starved in ill-nourished bodies a nation's children the stunted and silenced
the ill taught the taught not at all the slaughtered young who should be alive but aren't
who'll never lift out of their fearsome death of the soul he feels them hears them as they groan
through the darkness under their willfully unseeing country country willfully deaf to the death
pouring through it groaning and sighing beneath it its weapons and wars its moral obtuseness
he hears again those who died of their ignorance died of hatred of neglect hears their souls
as they writhe in their void he hears them *Not still Not again* all around him and the war
the wars *Not still Not again* that echo in each soul in a country ever at war he hears it

JUNK

So much junk so much waste so much discarded thrown away out of the world of attention
he hovers there in the void of old washers old dryers freezers cars their engines gone dead
televisions gone blind the heaters and coolers blowers and vacuums machines for making
other machines he hovers over the waste-holes driven into the earth chemical slops nuclear scum
grease so much surplus in a landscape of want and the humans the humans discarded in
   prisons
two million in prisons he counts them *two million in prisons* counts again two million
stacked up in absolute violence absolute terror absolute torpor two million coiled cocked
like rifles and how he thinks as he always has thought am I not myself junk when I see others
defined in their essence as junk those a culture by a process it can't itself understand decides
it can't afford to redeem can't in its infinite wealth find the wherewithal to lift out of their dark

GOVERNMENT

Where is he now he hears whispering voices murmuring he must be under the government
he hears the supposed voices of reason supposed murmurs of judicious analysis and reflection
but he knows as soon as he hears they're proclaiming what they've been proclaiming forever
go away leave go away and they do the fearful and timid the lost deceived all go away leave
the old frightened of losing their homes arrive then leave leave *Not still* he thinks *Not again*
and the new middle class falling back desperate to hold on to their homes the workers
   frightened
of losing their jobs go away their votes in their hands *Still Again* their blank suffering votes
crumpled and useless in their hands all go away as the government goes on with its whispering
its ravings its voices of deafness the voices always the same the illusion that government
believes its own delusion that it does anything more than murmur or rant to itself *Still Again*

MONEY

Underneath everything money under the government under the waste he still senses the money
it rots in boxes and bins and cases and cartons the money the mania for money for buying
and selling and profit and greed the rank passion for more the word itself "more" the purpose
always more so abysses are crammed with profits vaults flooded with profits and sometimes
if jobs must be cut so be it if the workforce downsized so be it and the factories closed down
the small merchants driven away so money can seep over and under ocean and mountain
he hears money move to the shores of cheap labor faceless amoral money flowing like lava
only the market knows best the wise market the theorists cry the cunningly conscious
benevolent market the congressmen and their lobbyists all driven by greed mindless heartless
for all now the heartless money with its infinite sinkholes of infinite greed *Oh still Oh again*

RAGE

The rage now he feels it the rage seeping down towards him like acid leaching frustration rage
indignation the misplaced overcompensated repressed of those who've lost and those fearful
of losing he can feel them strive for an answer and the only answer they find is rage *Still Again*
rage impatience and how tell them he thinks not to rage not to hold so to bitter resentment
and now the acids of rage sear in him too he feels it himself too his skin blistering with it in
    furies
of violence furies of fear his very flesh if he were still something of flesh would harden like leather
his body harden his soul harden he feels his soul becoming a thing like a bullet a shell a rocket
shrapnel explosives driven *Again* through the entrails of his country through him himself
deeper into the rage of his country the fearful insecure entrails of the fearfulness of his country
hardening in rage almost exploding the truth he once knew detonated by resentment and rage

Who he was who he is who they are the gestures of kindness gestures of love across gulfs
of confusion despite the anguish that tears him despite enmity malice rancor apathy weakness
despite the memory of hope too much hope he knows therefore too much acrid despair
he remembers remembers again the good hearts the mercy the pity the hope despite pain
flooding down like acid the pain of good hearts the pain of hearts charged with pity and peace
he remembers they were his children his wards that too *Still Again* there are the eyes the faces
one human being at a time white black yellow or brown it didn't matter *Still Again* now
and he knows if he could he'd go back even through the dark of cries of despair he'd go back
again through the torn cities back back no matter the money the pain and waste still he'd go
    back
something takes him away he feels himself crying but rising *Still Again* knows he'd go back

Either/Or

1.

My dream after the dream of more war: that for every brain
there exists a devil, a particular devil, hairy, scaly or slimy,
but compact enough to slot between lobes, and evil, implacably evil,
slicing at us from within, causing us to yield to the part
of the soul that argues itself to pieces, then reconstitutes as a club.

When I looked closely, though, at my world, it seemed to me devils
were insufficient to account for such terror, confusion, and hatred:
evil must be other than one by one, one at a time, it has to be general,
a palpable something like carbon dioxide or ash that bleeds
over the hemispheres of the world as over the halves of the mind.

But could it really be that overarching? What of love, generosity,
pity? So I concluded there after all would have to be devils,
but mine, when I dug through the furrows to find him, seemed listless,
mostly he spent his time honing his horns—little pronged things
like babies' erections, but sharp, sharp as the blade that guts the goat.

2.

Just as in the brain are devils, in the world are bees: bees are angels,
angels bees. Each person has his or her bee, and his or her angel,
not "guardian angel," not either one of those with ". . . drawn swords . . ."
who ". . . inflict chastisement . . ." but angels of presence, the presence
that flares in the conscience not as philosophers' fire, but bees'.

Bee-fire is love, angel-fire is too: both angels and bees evolve
from seen to unseen; both as you know from your childhood
have glittering wings but regarded too closely are dragons. Both,
like trappers, have fur on their legs, sticky with lickings of pollen:
for angels the sweetness is maddening; for bees it's part of the job.

Still, not in their wildest imaginings did the angel-bees reckon
to labor like mules, be trucked from meadow to mountain,
have their compasses fouled so they'd fall on their backs,
like old men, like me, dust to their diamond, dross to their ore,
but wondering as they do who in this cruel strew of matter will save us.

Two Movements for an Allegretto

BEETHOVEN, SYMPHONY NO. 7

1.

That dip in existence, that hollow, that falling-off place, cliff or abyss
where silence waits, lurks, hovers, beneath world, beneath sense;

that barren of stillness, hugely inert, waiting for us to surrender again,
give over our hardly heard mewling and braying to its implacable craw.

But now, abruptly, seemingly, too, from falling place, void or abyss,
that first chord, then, extruded from it yet somehow bringing along

the silence behind it, comes theme, then counter-theme, both keeping
within them the threat of regression back to devouring silence,

yet keeping us in them as well, so our dread of that vastness is calmed,
and we can respond, as though we'd been created, evolved to respond.

2.

That tangle, that weaving, that complicating in music and mind;
that counterpoint spun like a nest of filament, lichen, and down;

that magical no-longer-silence which takes us, is with us, is in us;
the roar of logic and the baying of our needs and desires all stilled,

and silence again is that hallowed place in the kingdom of being
where one note can change to the next, one key to another;

and in that shimmer we're brought back to the first silence,
but danced now, fugued now, ecstatically transfigured and vanquished,

so we can return to the primal chord that began this, begat this,
and brings this to its end; this exaltation, this splendor, this bliss.

I Hate

I hate how this unsummoned sigh-sound, sob-sound,
not sound really, feeling, sigh-feeling, sob-feeling,
keeps rasping in me, not in its old guise as nostalgia,
sweet crazed call of blackbird in spring;

not as remembrance, grief for so many gone;
nor either that other tangle of recall: regret
for unredeemed wrongs, errors, omissions,
petrified root too deeply hooked to ever excise;

a mingling rather, a melding, inextricable mesh
of delight in astonishing being, of being in being,
with a fear of and fear for I can barely think what,
not nonexistence, of self, loved ones, love;

not even war, fuck war, sighing for war,
sobbing for war, for no war, peace, surcease;
more than all that, some ground-sound, ground-note,
sown in us now, that swells in us, all of us,

echo of love we had, have, for world, our world,
on which we seem finally mere swarm, mere deluge,
mere matter self-altered to tumult, to noise,
cacophonous blitz of destruction, despoilment,

din from which every emotion henceforth emerges,
and into which falters, slides, sinks, and subsides:
sigh-sound of lament, of remorse; sob-sound of rue,
of, still, always, ever sadder and sadder sad joy.

Blackstone

When Blackstone the magician cut a woman in half in the Branford theater
near the famous Lincoln statue in already partway down the chute Newark,

he used a gigantic buzz saw, and the woman let out a shriek that outshrieked
the whirling blade and drilled directly into the void of our little boy crotches.

That must be when we learned that real men were supposed to hurt women,
make them cry then leave them, because we saw the blade go in, right in,

her waist was bare—look!—and so, in her silvery garlanded bra, shining,
were her breasts, oh round, silvery garlanded tops of breasts shining.

Which must be when we went insane, and were sent to drive our culture insane . . .
"Show me your breasts, please." *"Shame on you, hide your breasts—shame."*

Nothing else mattered, just silvery garlanded breasts, and still she shrieked,
the blade was still going in, under her breasts, and nothing else mattered.

Oh Branford theater, with your scabby plaster and threadbare scrim,
you didn't matter, and Newark, your tax base oozing away to the suburbs,

you didn't matter, nor your government by corruption, nor swelling slums—
you were invisible now, those breasts had made you before our eyes vanish,

as Blackstone would make doves then a horse before our eyes vanish,
as at the end factories and business from our vanquished city would vanish.

Oh Blackstone, gesturing, conjuring, with your looming, piercing glare.
Oh gleaming, hurtling blade, oh drawn-out scream, oh perfect, thrilling arc of pain.

Dust

Face powder, gunpowder, talcum of anthrax,
shavings of steel, crematoria ash, chips
of crumbling poetry paper—all these in my lockbox,
and dust, tanks, tempests, temples of dust.

Saw-, silk-, chalk-dust and chaff,
the dust the drool of a bull swinging its head
as it dreams its death
slobs out on; dust even from that scoured,

scraped littoral of the Aegean,
troops streaming screaming across it
at those who that day, that age or forever
would be foe, worthy of being dust for.

Last, hovering dust of the harvest, brief
as the half-instant hitch in the flight
of the hawk, as the poplets of light
through the leaves of the bronzing maples.

Animal dust, mineral, mental, all hoarded
not in the jar of sexy Pandora, not
in the ark where the dust of the holy aspiring
to congeal as glorious mud-thing still writhes—

just this leathery, crackled, obsolete box,
heart-sized or brain, rusted lock shattered,
hinge howling with glee to be lifted again . . .
Face powder, gunpowder, dust, darling dust.

The Foundation

Watch me, I'm running, watch me, I'm dancing, I'm air;
the building I used to live in has been razed and I'm skipping,
hopping, two-footedly leaping across the blocks, bricks,
slabs of concrete, plaster, and other unnameable junk . . .

Or nameable, really, if you look at the wreckage closely . . .
Here, for instance, this shattered I-beam is the Bible,
and this chunk of mortar? Plato, the mortar of mind,
also in pieces, in pieces in me, anyway, in my mind . . .

Aristotle and Nietzsche, Freud and Camus and Buber,
and Christ, even, that year of reading *Paradise Lost*,
when I thought, Hell, why not? but that fractured, too . . .
Kierkegaard, Hegel, and Kant, and Goffman and Marx,

all heaped in the foundation, and I've sped through so often
that now I have it by heart, can run, dance, be air,
not think of the spew of intellectual dust I scuffed up
when in my barely broken-in boots I first clumped through

the sanctums of Buddhism, Taoism, Zen, and the Areopagite,
even, whose entire text I typed out—my god, why?—
I didn't care, I just kept bumping my head on the lintels,
Einstein, the Gnostics, Kabbalah, Saint This and Saint That . . .

2.

Watch me again now, because I'm not alone in my dancing,
my being air, I'm with my poets, my Rilke, my Yeats,
we're leaping together through the debris, a jumble of wrack,
but my Keats floats across it, my Herbert and Donne,

my Kinnell, my Bishop and Blake are soaring across it,
my Frost, Baudelaire, my Dickinson, Lowell and Larkin,
and my giants, my Whitman, my Shakespeare, my Dante
and Homer; they were the steel, though scouring as I was

the savants and sages half the time I hardly knew it . . .
But Vallejo was there all along, and my Sidney and Shelley,
my Coleridge and Hopkins, there all along with their music,
which is why I can whirl through the rubble of everything else,

the philosophizing and theories, the thesis and anti- and syn-,
all I believed must be what meanings were made of,
when really it was the singing, the choiring, the cadence,
the lull of the vowels, the chromatical consonant clatter . . .

Watch me again, I haven't landed, I'm hovering here
over the fragments, the remnants, the splinters and shards;
my poets are with me, my soarers, my skimmers, my skaters,
aloft on their song in the ruins, their jubilant song of the ruins.

Jew on Bridge

Raskolnikov hasn't slept. For days. In his brain, something like white.
A wave stopped in mid-leap. Thick, slow, white. Or maybe it's brain.
Brain in his brain. Old woman's brain on the filthy floor of his brain.

His destiny's closing in. He's on his way, we're given to think, though
he'll have to go first through much suffering, to punishment, then redemption.
Love, too. Punishment, love, redemption; it's all mixed up in his brain.

Can't I go back to my garret, to my filthy oilcloth couch, and just sleep?
That squalid neighborhood where he lived. I was there. Whores, beggars,
derelict men with flattened noses: the police break their noses on purpose.

Poor crumpled things. He can't, though, go back to his filthy garret.
Rather this fitful perambulation. Now we come to a bridge on the Neva.
Could you see the sea from there then? I think I saw it from there.

Then, on the bridge, hanging out of the plot like an arm from a car,
no more function than that in the plot, car, window, arm, even less,
there, on the bridge, purposeless, plotless, not even a couch of his own: Jew.

On page something or other, chapter something, Raskolnikov sees JEW.
And takes a moment, a break, you might say, from his plot, from his fate,
his doom, to hate him, the Jew, loathe, despise, want him not *there*.

Jew. Not as in Chekhov's ensemble of Jews wailing for a wedding.
Not Chekhov, dear Chekhov. Dostoevsky instead, whom I esteemed
beyond almost all who ever scraped with a pen, but who won't give the Jew,

miserable Jew, the right to be short, tall, thin or fat Jew: just Jew.
Something to distract you from your shuttering tunnel of fate, your memory,
consciousness, loathing, self-loathing, knowing the slug you are.

What's the Jew doing anyway on that bridge on the beautiful Neva?
Maybe he's Paul, as in Celan. Antschel-Celan, who went over the rail of a bridge.
Oh my *Todesfugue*, Celan is thinking. The river's not the Neva, but the Seine.

It's the bridge on the Seine where Jew-poet Celan is preparing himself.
My *Deathfugue*. My black milk of daybreak. Death-master from Germany.
Dein goldenes Haar Marguerite. Dein aschenes Haar Sulamith. Aschenes-Antschel.

Was it sunrise, too, as when Raskolnikov, sleepless, was crossing his bridge?
Perhaps sleepless is why Raskolnikov hates this Jew, this Celan, this Antschel.
If not, maybe he'd love him. Won't he love the prisoners in his camp?

Won't he love and forgive and cherish the poor girl he's been tormenting?
Christian forgiveness all over the place, like brain on your boot.
Though you mustn't forgive, in your plot, Jew on bridge; *Deathfugue* on bridge.

Celan-Antschel goes over the rail. As have many others before him.
There used to be nets down near Boulogne to snare the debris, the bodies,
of prostitutes, bankrupts, sterile young wives, gamblers, and naturally Jews.

Celan was so sick of the *Deathfugue* he'd no longer let it be printed.
In the tape of him reading, his voice is songful and fervent, like a cantor's.
When he presented the poem to some artists, they hated the way he recited.

His parents had died in the camps. Of typhus the father. Mama probably gun.
Celan-Antschel, had escaped. He'd tried to convince them to come, too.
Was that part of it, on the bridge? Was that he wrote in German part, too?

He stood on the bridge over the Seine, looked into the black milk of dying,
Jew on bridge, and hauled himself over the rail. *Dein aschenes Haar* . . .
Dostoevsky's Jew, though, is still there. On page something or other.

He must be waiting to see where destiny's plotting will take him. It won't.
He'll just have to wait there forever. Jew on bridge, hanging out of the plot.
I try to imagine what he would look like. My father? Grandfathers? Greats?

Does he wear black? Would he be like one of those hairy Hasids
where Catherine buys metal for her jewelry, in their black suits and hats,
even in summer, *shvitzing*, in the heat? Crackpots, I think. They depress me.

Do I need forgiveness for my depression? My being depressed like a Jew?
All right then: how Jewish am I? What portion of who I am is a Jew?
I don't want vague definitions, qualifications, here on the bridge of the Jew.

I want certainty, *science*: everything you are, do, think; think, do, are,
is precisely twenty-two percent Jewish. Or six and a half. Some nice prime.
Your suffering is Jewish. Your resistant, resilient pleasure in living, too,

can be tracked to some Jew on some bridge on page something or other
in some city, some village, some shtetl, some festering *shvitz* of a slum,
with Jews with black hats or not, on their undershirts fringes or not.

Raskolnikov, slouching, shoulders hunched, hands in his pockets,
stinking from all those sleepless nights on his couch, clothes almost rotting,
slouching and stinking and shivering and muttering to himself, plods on

past the Jew on the bridge, who's dressed perhaps like anyone else—
coat, hat, scarf, boots—whatever. Our hero would recognize him
by his repulsive, repellent Jew-face daring to hang out in the air.

My father's name also was Paul. As in Celan. His father's name: Benjamin.
As in Walter. Who flung himself from life, too, with vials of morphine.
In some hotel from which he could have reached safety but declined to.

Chose not to. Make it across. Though in fact none of us makes it across.
Aren't we all in that same shitty hotel on that bridge in the shittiest world?
What was he thinking, namesake of my grandpa? Benjamin, Walter, knew all.

Past, future, all. He could see perfectly clearly the death he'd miss out on.
You're in a room. Dark. You're naked. Crushed on all sides by others naked.
Flesh-knobs. Hairy or smooth. Sweating against you. *Shvitzing* against you.

Benjamin would have played it all out in his mind like a fugue. *Deathfugue.*
The sweating, the stinking. And that moment you know you're going to die,
and the moment past that, which, if you're Benjamin, Walter, not grandpa,

you know already by heart: the searing through you you realize is your grief,
for humans, all humans, their world and their cosmos and oilcloth stars.
All of it worse than your fear and grief for your own minor death.

So, gulp down the morphine quickly, because of your shame for the humans,
what humans can do to each other. Benjamin, grandfather, Walter;
Paul, father, Celan: all the names that ever existed wiped out in shame.

Celan on his bridge. Raskolnikov muttering Dostoevsky under his breath.
Jew on bridge. Raskolnikov-Dostoevsky still in my breath. Under my breath.
Black milk of daybreak. *Aschenes Haar.* Antschel-Celan. Ash. Breath.

From

Writers Writing Dying

(2012)

Whacked

Every morning of my life I sit at my desk getting whacked by some great poet or other.
Some Yeats, some Auden, some Herbert or Larkin, and lately a whole tribe of others—
oi!—younger than me. *Whack!* Wiped out, every day . . . I mean since becoming a poet.
I mean wanting to—one never is, really, a poet. Or I'm not. Not when I'm trying to write,
though then comes a line, maybe another, but still pops up again Yeats, say, and again *whacked*.

. . . Wait . . . Old brain in my head, I'd forgotten that "whacked" in crime movies means
  murdered,
rubbed out, by the mob—little the mob-guys would think that poets could do it, and who'd
  believe
that instead of running away you'd find yourself fleeing *towards* them, some sweet-seeming
  Bishop
who's saying *so*—*so*—*so*, but *whack!* you're stampeding again through her poems like a
  mustang,
whacked so hard that you bash the already-broken crown of your head on the roof of your stall.

. . . What a relief to read for a while some bad poems. Still, I try not to—bad, whackless poems
can hurt you, can say you're all right when you're not, can condone your poet-coward
who compulsively asks if you're all right—*Am I all right?*—not wasting your time—
Am I wasting time?—though you know you are, wasting time, if you're not being *whacked*.
Bad poems let you off that: the confessional mode now: I've read reams, I've written as many.

Meanwhile, this morning, this very moment, I'm thinking of George Herbert composing;
I see him, by himself, in some candlelit chamber unbearably lonely to us but glorious to him,
and he's hunched over, scribbling, scribbling, and the room's filling with poems whacking at me,
and Herbert's not even paying attention as the huge tide of them rises and engulfs me
in warm tangles of musical down as from the breasts of the choiring dawn-tangling larks.

"Lovely enchanting language, sugar-cane . . ." Whack! *"The sweet strains, the lullings . . ."*
Oh whack! Lowell or Keats, Rilke or Wordsworth or Wyatt: whack—fifty years of it,
old racehorse, plug hauling its junk—isn't it time to be put out to pasture? But, ah, I'd still
if I could lie down like a mare giving birth, arm in my own uterine channel to tug out another,
one more, only one more, poor damp little poem, then I'll be happy—I promise, I swear.

A Hundred Bones

In this mortal frame of mine, which consists of a hundred bones and nine orifices, there is something, and this something can be called, for lack of a better name, a windswept spirit . . .
BASHŌ

And thus the hundred bones of my body plus various apertures plus that thing I don't know yet
to call spirit are all aquake with joyous awe at the shriek of the fighter planes that from their base
at Port Newark swoop in their practice runs so low over our building that the walls tremble.

Wildcats, they're called, Thunderbolts or Corsairs, and they're practicing *strafing*, which in war means
your machine guns are going like mad as you dive down on the enemy soldiers and other bad people,
Nips, Krauts, trying to run out from under your wings, your bullet-pops leaping after their feet.

It's a new word for us, *strafing*. We learn others, too: *blockbusters*, for instance, which means
bombs that smash down your whole block: not our block, some *Nip* block, or *Nazi*—
some gray block in the newsreel. B-24 is the number of my favorite bomber: the Liberator.

My best fighter: *Lightning*. The other kind of lightning once crashed on an eave of our building
and my mother cried out and swept me up in her arms: *The war is here*, she must have thought,
the war has found me. All her life I think she was thinking: *The war is here, the war has found me.*

Some words we don't know yet—*gas chamber, napalm*—children our age, in nineteen forty-four, say,

say my friend Arnold and I, who're discussing how we'll torture our treacherous enemy-friends who've gone off to a ball game without us. They're like enemies, Japs or Nazis: so of course torture.

Do children of all places and times speak so passionately and knowledgeably about torture? Our imaginations are small, though, Arnold's and mine. Tear out their nails. Burn their eyes. Drive icicles in their ear so there's no evidence of your having done it except they're dead.

Then it was Arnold who died. He was a doctor, out west; he learned to fly Piper Cubs, and flew out to help Navajo women have babies. He'd become a good man. Then he was dead. But right now: victory! V-Day! Clouds like giant ice creams over the evil Japanese empire.

Cities are burning. Some Japanese cities aren't even there. *The war is here! The war has found me!*
Japanese poets come later. We don't know we need them until they're already buffing the lens. Bashō. Issa. Buson. Especially Basho: ah, that *windswept spirit*; ah, that hardly-there frog.

Atom bomb, though: Bashō as shadow burned into asphalt. House torn by mad burning wind. Poets in coats of straw, burning. What is our *flaw*, we human beings? What is our *error*? Spikes in your tushy, ice in your brain. That frog invisibly waiting forever to make its leap.

Vile Jelly

I see they're tidying the Texas textbooks again.
Chopping them down to make little minds stay
the right size for the preachers not to be vexed
as they troll for converts, or congregants, or whatever.

Troll. As in "Fish for Men." As in ". . . for Christ."
Here's a fisher: a pre-biblical king on a slab. Captives.
The king with a not-sharp spear is blinding the first,
thrusting then twisting it into the writhing man's eye.

Subtle carvers they were: you see the thrust and twist.
How the hook, the *fish hook*, driven through the lip
of the victim to keep him from inconveniently struggling
and attached to a rope, tugs the lip out from the teeth.

Because the whole state of Texas buys the same book,
the import of their distortions and falsehoods is wide.
The publishers take them into account,
so other states' schoolbooks are dumbed down as well.

Who said: *With my eyes closed, I see more*? Not me.
Who said: *I study not to learn but hoping
what I've learned might not be true*? Not me again.
I stay still. I peek warily out the door of my stove.

That's a story about seeing, not having to see.
A fairy tale with your usual prince, this time in a stove.
It doesn't say why he's there, even after he's saved,
by your usual virgin. The scholars don't explain either.

My theory is he locked himself in, welded the lid,
because of all he could no longer bear to behold.
Texas textbooks, for instance. Chunks of knowledge
extracted like eyes. Discarded. Thrown on a floor.

Evolution, needless to say. Sociology. Jefferson. Deism.
All these complications henceforth won't vex.
They'll be scraped from the mold. No longer be *seen*.
As much is no longer seen in the world as well.

Will the eyes of conscience also be punctured? Spilled?
Vile jelly, it's called in *King Lear*. Vile jelly. *Out.*
"Chips of blank," Dickinson wrote in a war poem.
"Chips of blank in boyish eyes." Is that still in the books?

Is the king on the slab with his spear and rope?
But that was before Christ rose. Into his own stove.
"The noise of mankind," another god groused,
"is too loud, they keep me awake. Rid me of them."

The underling angels began boiling the acid,
but thanks be someone had learned how to write.
An inscription appeared on a roof.
Please, it pled to the prickly deity, *don't.*

And the almighty, yawning after for once a good nap,
decided to let us do it unto ourselves.
Which we're rushing to do. As quick as we can.
By making the mysteries holy and blank.

By chopping eyes from susceptible minds.
Susceptible hearts. Thou vilest jelly.
Herds of children go bleeding into the dark.
Oh, vile. Thou chips of blank. Thou boyish eyes.

Bianca Burning

The sexual terror lions are roaring into my ears as I make my way between their cages
at the Bertram Mills Circus in England in nineteen fifty-seven when I'm twenty.
The terrible lions have roared for six months and though I don't know it they'll roar
for six more then be extinguished, leaving only their irksome echo the rest of my life.

A circus—I'm traveling with a *circus*, an exotic thing to think, and I have a Bianca—
not the Bianca Bruno Schulz had in his "Spring," an "enchanting" Bianca whom one
"would notice . . . how with every step light as a dancer she enters her being . . ."—a Bianca,
rather, who's lush, ardent, and, though only eighteen, more amorously advanced than I am,

with breasts too beautiful to remember and that other thing farther down she'll bring
with her every day to my "digs" to roll with me on my bed, while I flail and despair,
and return with her back through that savage alley, that gauntlet of error and terror,
to the "caravan" where her father and mother lived, and where we ate dinner together.

Bianca's father is a clown. Not the way I was a clown, a sexual clown, not the way
Schulz depicts himself in his drawings as almost a clown, with his rack of compulsions—
Bianca's father's a real clown, famous, with different names in different countries,
who in the ring in his Chaplinesque costume is hilarious, reckless, contagiously joyful.

Yet Bianca's father like me is possessed by a terror, though no one dares frame it that way.
Bianca's mother, you see, has claustrophobia, a terrible case, and it was agreed
that for her to sleep in their cramped trailer would be painful, insupportable really,
so Bianca's beautiful mother, lusher even than Bianca, and so young seen from here,

younger than my daughter now, would kiss her impassive, pipe-smoking husband
and leave in the car that came every night to take her to the circus owner's yacht,
and we remnants, we relics, would gloomily sit; Bianca because soon she'd have to go
back to her job as a nightclub dancer, and the husband, for obvious reasons, and me,

part of the act now, with my rituals of desire and my dread of the lions I'll pass again
as I wend the torturous route to my room to wait for Bianca's next visit tomorrow,
with her breasts, and that other thing which I could hardly bring myself in those days
to call by its name, so fearsome it was, as it was for the tragic and timid Schulz,

who even in his erotic etchings of perfectly formed nudes with Schulz-like men
abjectly groveling, crushed, dejected, under their elegant feet, depicts no vaginas,
or none not submerged in inkiest shadow, save one, and that sketchy, inconsequential,
which surely proves that Schulz knew the firmament of vagina is fathomless,

without measurable dimensions, altering such shape it does have with impatience,
but for which Schulz's Bianca, who "controlled her glamour with pity,"
and whose wisdom was "full of sadness," must by now offer demure consolation,
while mine, my Bianca, struts with top hat and whip across the arena to take her bow.

Rat Wheel, Dementia, Mont Saint-Michel

FOR ALBERT O. HIRSCHMAN

My last god's a theodicy glutton, a good-evil gourmet—
peacock and plague, gene-junk; he gobbles it down.
Poetry, violence; love, war—his stew of honey and thorn.

For instance, thinks theodicy-god: Mont Saint-Michel.
Sheep, sand, steeple honed sharp as a spear. And inside,
a contraption he calls with a chuckle the rat wheel.

Thick timber three meters around, two persons across,
into which prisoners were inserted to trudge, toil,
hoist food for the bishop and monks; fat bishop himself.

The wheel weighs and weighs. You're chained in; you toil.
Then they extract you. Where have your years vanished?
What difference? says theodicy-god. Wheel, toil: what difference?

Theodicy-god has evolved now to both substance and not.
With handy metaphysical blades to slice brain meat from mind.
For in minds should be voidy wings choiring, not selves.

This old scholar, for instance, should have to struggle to speak,
should not remember his words, paragraphs, books:
that garner of full-ripened grain must be hosed clean.

Sometimes as the rat wheel is screaming, theodicy-god
considers whether to say he's sorry: that you can't speak,
can't remember your words, paragraphs, books.

Sorry, so sorry. *Blah*, his voice thinks instead, *blah*.
He can't do it. Best hope instead they'll ask him again
as they always do for forgiveness. But what if they don't?

What might have once been a heart feels pity, for itself though,
not the old man with no speech—for him and his only scorn.
Here in my rat wheel, my Mont Saint-Michel, my steeple of scorn.

Exhaust

My grandson wants a *Ferrari*. I buy one for him. Why not?
The second a *Mercedes*. The third a *Porsche*. Why not?
How things change—my grandfather wanted only the pickup
one icy Rochester night the year before I was born
he skidded through a gate in and plowed head-on into a train.

My grandsons' cars cost a dollar, part of a vast collection
of racers, convertibles, trucks, even antiques from the time
I had my first car, a five-year-old ungainly green *Chevy*,
not like Lowell's father's spanking new one—"with gilded hooves,"
wrote Lowell, and, slashingly, "his best friend."

I treasured my *Chevy*, too, though it plodded compared with
a friend's *Olds* that sped us one New Year's Eve
after the parties down the parkway at a hundred and ten.
My grandfather I gather was vain of his truck, and his driving,
but my grandmother would grumble, "He was a terrible driver."

We were good drivers, we were certain, better than good—
didn't we all but live in our cars? Wasn't the best part even
of a date when you made out with your girlfriend in back?
Right now, hitting *a hundred*, don't we love each other
for how our tires are glued to the pavement and life has no end?

I hadn't seen Warhol's print yet of mangled teenagers
spilled from their wreck. I didn't see much then beyond cars,
like my grandsons, who know every make, model,
top speed, and zero to sixty by heart, and who'll squabble
because one has stolen another's X-something or other.

My grandfather was a socialist when that word still could be used.
He even ran for state senate, though not surprisingly lost—
he was hardly well-off, with a store that sold candy and papers,
and why he needed that broken-down truck, my grandmother
still complained on her deathbed, was a mystery to her.

The first time I was almost killed in a car, an axle sheared,
our back wheel bounced past us, we spun out of control
over a busy highway, and pulled up a yard from a tree,
much like the tree in the photo of the death of Camus
with his publisher's sports car gruesomely wrapped around it.

Such a short time between my automobile madness
and my rapture reading Camus—*Sisyphus* telling me why
suicide wasn't the route, though at the time it could seem so.
What did he say exactly? I don't think there was much about love,
which would be my reason now: love, family, poetry, art.

I sometimes imagined my *Chevy* was devoted to me, like a dog.
That was before death arrived; mine and everyone else's.
Anne Sexton's father died in a car: dear Anne made certain to, too.
Pollock, Sebald, Nathanael West; *Tom Mix*, for god's sake;
me nearly four times, and my grandfather Charles Kasdin.

Whom I just realized now I miss, and whom if I'd been there
I know I could have saved: *Pump the brakes gently*, I'd tell him,
and we'd glide up to the rails, and wait in the beautiful snow.
He'd offer some wisdom to hand on to my grandsons,
the train clattering by us, the mingling steam of our breath.

Butchers

1.

Thank goodness we were able to wipe the Neanderthals out, beastly things,
from our mountains, our tundra—that way we had all the meat we might need.

Thus the butcher can display under our eyes his scrubbed hands on the block,
and never refer to the rooms hidden behind where dissections are effected,

where flesh is reduced to its shivering atoms and remade for our delectation
as cubes, cylinders, barely material puddles of admixtured horror and blood.

Rembrandt knew of all this—isn't his flayed beef carcass really a caveman?
It's Christ also, of course, but much more a troglodyte such as we no longer are.

Vanished those species—begone!—those tribes, those peoples, those nations—
Myrmidon, Ottoman, Olmec, Huron, and Kush: gone, gone, and goodbye.

2.

But back to the chamber of torture, to Rembrandt, who was telling us surely
that hoisted with such cables and hung from such hooks we, too, would reveal

within us intricate layerings of color and pain: alive the brush is with pain,
aglow with the cruelties of crimson, the cooled, oblivious ivory of our innards.

Fling out the hooves of your hands! Open your breast, pluck out like an Aztec
your heart howling its Cro-Magnon cries that compel to battles of riddance!

Our own planet at last, where purged of wilderness, homesickness, prowling,
we're no longer compelled to devour our enemies' brains, thanks to our butcher,

who inhabits this palace, this senate, this sentried barbed-wire enclosure
where dare enter none but subservient breeze; bent, broken blossom; dry rain.

Haste

Not so fast people were always telling me *Slow down take your time* teachers coaches
the guy who taught me to ride (*"Stop cowboying"* he'd shout as if that wasn't the point)

but the admonition that stuck was the whisper that girl that woman that smudged now
dear girl-woman legs so tightly wound round me sighed young as she was to my ear

Ah the celestial contraption we made though—no matter how you swerved it it held together
Why not go faster? But she with her fluttery guttural *Slower go slower* knew better knew better

No one says *Not so fast* now not Catherine when I hold her not our dog as I putter behind her
yet everything past present future rushes so quickly through me I've frayed like a flag

Unbuckle your spurs life don't you know up ahead where the road ends there's an abyss?
No room for galloping anymore here Surely by now you should know better know better

Poem for Myself for My Birthday

It's coming at me again, damn, like that elephant with its schoonering ears charging in Uganda.

We were okay, we thought, in our Rover, so it was a nice mix of scary and thrilling, plus a story
to tell—

that behemoth, Wow! snorting a few yards off in the bush, waving his huge crushing tusks.

Then rushing out at us. At us. Like my birthday. Like thinking of birthdays, this one, the next,

the next to last and—ouch—the last, all stampeding towards me like that most likely ill
outlaw,

ponderous-looking but so fast on his feet you can't even dream of dancing out of the way.

Out of the way! Step on the gas! Okay, we're out of there, safe! . . . Wait, though, I'm not safe,

this time my birthday's a tractor trailer skidding sideways on ice and I'm noodling by on my
bike,

my darling old Raleigh, and the whole frame's pretzeled around me. Happy birthday? Oh,
please.

My last happy was that first one with a party—gooey brown cake and four beautiful candles.

And they're singing, to me! Even now it seems worth having lost one of my not-enough years.

I loved being sung to. And how not love that song? Especially ". . . to you!" To be "you" in a
song!

Now I'm often "you" to myself. You selfish bastard, you indolent slug. When did that happen?

I see the Dalai Lama's birthday's here, too; in his photo, he pumps a treadmill like a prayer
wheel,

and proclaims (boasts? admits?), "I visualize my death every day." I wonder if he's "you" to
himself?

Speaking of visualization: Yash Glatshteyn has a poem, "For My Two Hundredth Birthday,"
where he "talks of words" with friends in the garden, then makes love to his "soft, obedient
   maid."
Very sweet, nostalgia for the future, ingenious device when your present's all but used up.

But forget the meshugeneh future, I can't even get the past straight: everything keeps popping
   up changed.
It's like being, not being in, *being*, one of those movies that starts with a flash forward, then—
   poof!—
the plot's rushed ahead and you're still back where you began and way out here near the end.

Did Glatshteyn's wife ever forgive him that succulent poem-maid? Catherine would go crazy.
No problem for the celibate Dalai Lama, though I'd bet there've been enough "maids" he could
   have . . .
Well, slept with, the way Gandhi slept with young girls when he was old—to keep warm, he
   avowed.

As did King David. All those thank-you notes to be written, those apology calls. You liar. You
   cheat.
Happy Birthday to me. Dalai Lama and me. By now that poor stricken elephant's probably
   dead.
To him, too, Happy Returns. And me, spinning by on my bike, singing, "To you; oh, to you."

Salt

Abashingly eerie that just because I'm here on the long low-tide beach of age with briny time
licking insidious eddies over my toes there'd rise in me those mad weeks a lifetime ago
when I had two lovers, one who soaked herself so in *Chanel* that before I went to the other
I'd scrub with fistfuls of salt and not only would the stink be vanquished but I'd feel shame-
    shriven, pure,
which thinking about is a joke: how not acknowledge—obsolete notion or no—that I was a
    cad.

Luckily though, I've hung onto my Cornell box of pastness with its ten thousand compart-
    ments,
so there's a place for these miniature mountains of salt, each with its code-tag of amnesia,
and also for the flock of Donnas and Ednas and Annies, a resplendent feather from each,
and though they're from the times I was not only crass, stupid, and selfish but thoughtless—
art word for shitty—their beaks open now not to berate but stereophonically warble for-
    giveness.

Such an engrossing contrivance: up near a corner, in tinsel, my memory moon, still glowing,
still cruel, because of the misery it magnified the times *I* was abandoned—"They flee . . . oh
    they flee . . ."
I'd abrade myself then not with salt but anapests, iambs, enjambments, and here they still are,
burned in in ink, but here, too, dead center, Catherine, with her hand-carved frame in a
    frame—
like the hero in Westerns who arrives just in time to rescue the town she galloped up to
    save me.

Well, I suppose soon the lid with its unpickable latch will come down, but the top I hope will
    be glass,

see-through, like Cornell's, so I'll watch myself for a while boinging around like a pinball, still loving this flipper-thing life that so surprisingly cannoned me up from oblivion's ramp, and to which I learned to sing in my own voice but sometimes thanks be in the voice of others, which is why I can croon now, "My lute be still . . ." and why I can cry, ". . . for I have done."

The Day Continues Lovely

With *Fear and Trembling* I studied my Kierkegaard, with *Sickness unto Death*
I contemplated with him my spiritual shortcomings, and it didn't occur to me
until now that in the Kierkegaard I've read he never takes time to actually pray.
Odd . . . This isn't to question his faith—who'd dare?—but his . . . well, agenda.
All those intricate paradoxes of belief he devotes his time to untying, retying.
Can it be that Kierkegaard simply *forgets* to pray, he's so busy untying, retying?
I understand that: I have times I forget to remember I can't pray. *Can't. Pray.*

This June morning just after sparkling daybreak and here I'm not praying.
My three grandsons asleep on their mats on the floor of my study,
shining, all three, more golden than gold, and I'm still not. *Not praying.*
Why aren't I? Even our dog Bwindi sprawled beside Turner, the youngest,
Turner's sleep-curled fist on her back: Why haven't I prayed about them?
I can imagine someday something inside me saying: *Well, why don't you?*
Something inside me. As though suddenly would be *something inside me.*

There's a Buber story I'm probably misrepresenting that touches on this.
A rabbi spends endless hours deciding whether to do good deeds or pray.
He thinks this first, then that: *This might be good; maybe that would be better*,
and suddenly a VOICE that can only be God's erupts: *STOP DAWDLING!*
And *God*, he thinks: he's been chastised by *God. STOP DAWDLING!*
And what happens then? In my anti-Bubering of the tale, everything's lost,
the fool's had his moment with God—even Moses had only how many?—

and he's squandered it because all he could do was stand stunned,
mouth hung metaphorically open, losing his chance to ask for guidance,
but he'd vacillated again and *What happens now?* he wonders in anguish.

Maybe I should get out of this business, find a teaching job, write a book,
on my desolation, my suffering, then he hears again, louder, *STOP! STOP!*
but this time it's his own voice, hopelessly loud, and he knows he'll forever be
in this waiting, this without-God, his glimpse of the Undeniable already waning.

And what about me? Leave aside Kierkegaard, Buber, the rabbis—just me.
Haven't I spent my life trying to make up my mind about *something*?
God, not God; soul, not soul. I'm like the Binary Kid: on, off; off, on.
But isn't that what we all are? Overgrown electrical circuits? Good, bad.
Hate, love. We go crazy trying to gap the space between on and off,
but there is none. Click. Click. Left: Right. Humans kill one another
because there's no room to maneuver inside those minuscule switches.

Meanwhile cosmos roars with so many voices we can't hear ourselves think.
Galaxy on. Galaxy off. Universe on, but another just behind this one,
one more out front waiting for us to be done. They're flowing across us,
sweet swamps of being—and we thrash in them, waving our futile antennae.
. . . Turner's awake now. He smiles, stands; Bwindi yawns and stands, too.
They come to see what I'm doing. Turner leans his head on my shoulder to peek.
What *am* I doing? Thinking of Kierkegaard. Thinking of beauty. Thinking of prayer.

Writers Writing Dying

Many I could name but won't who'd have been furious to die while they were sleeping but did—
outrageous, they'd have lamented, and never forgiven the death they'd construed for themselves
being stolen from them so rudely, so crudely, without feeling themselves like rubber gloves
stickily stripped from the innermostness they'd contrived to hoard for so long—all of it gone,
squandered, wasted, on what? *Death*, crashingly boring as long as you're able to think and
    write it.

Think, write, write, think: just keep running faster and you won't even notice you're dead.
The hard thing's when you're not thinking or writing and as far as you know you *are* dead
or might as well be, with no word for yourself, just that suction-shush like a heart pump or straw
in a milk shake and death which once wanted only to be sung back to sleep with its tired old
    fangs
has me in its mouth!—and where the hell are you that chunk of dying we used to call Muse?

Well, dead or not, at least there was that fancy, of some scribbler, some think-and-write person,
maybe it was yourself, soaring in the sidereal void, and not only that, you were holding a banjo
and gleefully strumming, and singing, jaw swung a bit under and off to the side the way crazily
happily people will do it—singing songs or not even songs, just lolly-molly syllable sounds
and you'd escaped even from language, from having to gab, from having to write down the idiot
    gab.

But in the meantime isn't this what it is to be dead, with that Emily-fly buzzing over your snout
that you're singing almost as she did; so what matter if you died in your sleep or rushed towards
    dying
like the Sylvia-Hart part of the tribe who ceased too quickly to be and left out some stanzas?
You're still aloft with your banjoless banjo, and if you're dead or asleep who really cares?
Such fun to wake up, though! Such fun, too, if you don't! Keep dying! Keep writing it down!

From

All at Once

(2014)

The Last Circus

The horse trainer's horse is a scrawny pony; its ribs show, and when it levers itself onto its battered pedestal, it looks more arthritic than I am. It's trained to nod its head "Yes," but you can tell it wouldn't care if what it's saying is "No," or "Never," or "Leave me alone, please."

His master also plays the clown—when he does, he looks like an accountant down on his luck: he's not very funny, we clap because we want him to be. He also juggles, though he keeps dropping the dumbbells and balls.

The girl who walks the tightrope, three feet off the ground, must be his daughter. Then she's the girl hanging from a long rope her clown-father swings; he lets her plummet down until her face nearly touches the sawdust, then she pops to her feet. Her costume is blotchy, and sags.

Intermission: behind the tent, the most bored lions in the world laze in their fetid cage, refusing to meet our eyes. Then a clutch of battered trailers, clotheslines slung from them out to some trees: T-shirts, towels, underclothes worn all but to air. Scattered beneath are crumpled pizza boxes, plastic bags, beer bottles, cans, other indecipherable junk.

The show begins again, the sparse audience climbs back onto the bleachers. One man sits engulfed by his children: a sleeping two-year-old sprawls across his lap, her head lolling on his shoulder; he kicks her gooey, half-eaten, half-melted glop of cotton candy into the void beneath; a larger child, another girl, sits on one of his knees, wriggling with delight, her circus banner waving in his face; and the last, a baby in the crook of his arm, he manages with the same hand that holds it to offer it some cola in a cup. A little dribbles on the baby's chin, and with a corner of his shirt he wipes it up, pats the disconsolate infant in his lap, who's just woken crying, and then, when the clown appears again, he cheers, stamps, whistles, and, like Shiva, foliates another pair of hands and heartily applauds.

Silence

The heron methodically pacing like an old-time librarian down the stream through the patch of woods at the end of the field, those great wings tucked in as neatly as clean sheets, is so intent on keeping her silence, extracting one leg, bending it like a paper clip, placing it back, then bending the other, the first again, that her concentration radiates out into the listening world, and everything obediently hushes, the ragged grasses that rise from the water, the light-sliced vault of sparkling aspens.

Then abruptly a flurry, a flapping, her lifting from the gravitied earth, her swoop out over the field, her banking and settling on a lightning-stricken oak, such a gangly, unwieldy contraption up there in the barkless branches, like a still Adam's-appled adolescent; then the cry, cranky, coarse, and wouldn't the waiting world laugh aloud if it could with glee?

The Two Voices of Elizabeth Bishop

On the same tape, the two voices: the younger, pert, perky, so early on already suffused with knowledge, it's tempting to say wisdom—though is knowledge wisdom? Then the later: a voice striated with the grittiness of time, of experience; the tone touched, just touched, by weariness, though with enough self-deprecation to indicate a really not overly debilitating weight of regret.

Young, imparting those blossomings of imagination the voice perhaps a little taken aback to have generated. Later, older: I did this, yes, it made some difference once, but I can't be bothered to remember what or when it would have been, though I still know it's there some-where, and I still esteem it.

In neither voice is there any indication of the timbre being afflicted by tears, both as shriven of such matters as are their verse. There's only an echo of tears' deepest origins, the chamber beneath voice from which arise not only tears but everything else.

If there's early on a wide-eyed pride along with wonder at having accomplished what has been accomplished, in the later it's gone. Though there's still a tinge, a touch, a hint of satis-faction, perhaps brought about by the sheer inescapability of knowing what she's wrought, there's no residual narcissistic pride, except perhaps a tiny bit, layered deep within the jokey prosy preludes to the reading of the poems themselves.

Gone completely is the urgency of the younger, the barely suppressed rush, hurry, the need to bring forth, have brought forth, more, more. Enduring, the self-astonished patience that sanctioned it all.

The Broom

The wide-bristled brooms that late at night in bus stations glide noiselessly over the terrazzo floors, as though they'd achieved the most intimate, unintimidated relation to duration, to time; as though, despite the tired salesman half asleep on a bench, the two college-kid lovers impatiently waiting in the dark sanctity of a Greyhound for the bus to depart so they can continue their furtive petting, the group of Asian women who huddle around a pay phone, listening, listening, waiting, hanging up then dialing again an instant later (what betrayal might they be involved in, what abandonment, desertion?), and the semi-winos and the semi-paranoid who are allowed to slump and sleep in these sanctuaries reserved for them, as well as we who are blessèd by the scriptures of our tickets—as though all of this might be systematically transcended, lifted from the precincts of a mere motorless implement patterning methodically over trivial shining expanses with a mad geometrical exactness, to a process more comprehensive, a tractor, say, in a wheat field after harvest, when every centimeter must be disked and harrowed, and all beneath a brutal August sun none of us trapped here has beheld for centuries, only fancied, dreamed of, here in this hallowed, middle place of bland fluorescent longing.

Manure

A winter's worth of manure towering in the yard beside the stable. A winter's worth of stable warmth rising in the chilly early April air. I walk to the gate, lift the crude wire latch to let the still thick-furred foal into the meadow, then go through into the paddock. A breeze winds down through the stand of pines on the hill, a rooster releases its garbled call to the waking world.

This never happened to me, yet it's memory, too, thrashing in its pathetic confining containers of truth, avid to evoke pasts it was never privileged to possess, to elate itself with nostalgia for moments of other lives.

... In this case the boys I knew who lived in the country, the children of farmers, horse breeders, blacksmiths, and my friends whose father taught in the city but came back every night to their summer camp in rural New Jersey to his wife and two sons who'd grown up there.

I envied the sons their life in the country. I wasn't even jealous of how at home they were in the fields and woods and barns; of how they could do so many things I couldn't, drive tractors, take apart and fix motors, pluck eggs from under a hen, shove their way into a stall with a stubborn horse pushing back: I just marveled at it all, and wanted it. They and the boys who lived on farms near them were also so enviably at ease in their bodies: what back in the city would be taken as a slouch of disinterest, here was an expression of physical grace. No need to be tense when everything so readily submitted to your efficiently minimal gestures: hoisting bales of hay into a loft, priming a recalcitrant pump ...

Something else there was as well, something more elusive: perhaps that they lived so much of the time in a world of wild, poignant odors—mown grass, the redolent pines, even the tang of manure and horse-piss-soaked hay. Just the thought of those sensory elations inflicted me with a feeling I still have to exert myself to repress that I was squandering my time, wasting what I knew already were irretrievable clutches of years, now hecatombs of years, trapped in my trivial, stifling life.

The Sign Painter

The summer camp where I worked as a headwaiter when I was sixteen hired men off the Bowery in New York as its kitchen staff. When a position would come open, which was often because one of the men was always falling off the wagon and vanishing, the owner would go down to the city and come back with yet another derelict soul. Some of them lasted awhile; one, a chef, very gruff, standoffish, who never spoke to anyone when he didn't have to, kept going all summer.

Another, a slight, self-effacing middle-aged man, was hired as a dishwasher, but when the camp owner discovered he had once been a sign painter, he commissioned him to paint the camp logo on their station wagon in his spare time. I don't know whether he'd brought his brush and paints with him, or whether they'd bought them for him, but every day after lunch he'd be hunched on a stool with his slender brushes and the rod with a little ball on the end he used to steady his hand, painstakingly painting the logo—it was a hawk, I had no idea why—along with the name of the camp in ornate lettering.

I liked him and was bored by camp life, so I used to sit with him and watch him work, and I became something like his confidant, maybe because I paid attention to what he was doing, which no one else did. He worked remarkably carefully, slowly, I suspected too slowly: though he obviously knew his craft, I guessed that his almost obsessional meticulousness must have been an impediment to whatever chance he'd have had of doing this as a profession. Or perhaps it was the other way around: perhaps this had been his profession, and he'd left it because his life had collapsed, sent him to drink, then to the streets, and, wounded, he could only work this way now.

One afternoon, after I'd been watching him for a while, he started to tell me about his past. I don't remember all that much, but there was a period he'd spent working, or maybe it was just making bets, at racetracks, and he made it sound like the high point of his life. Whatever the details were, it didn't matter much to me—I realized he was offering me the sense of an existence of which I had absolutely no inkling: he was offering me his life itself, and I knew even then to be moved and grateful.

I've wondered why he'd chosen me: I was a naïve, sheltered adolescent, and all I can think of is that there must have been something about me that was so unthreatening that he was able to talk about himself in a way he certainly wouldn't have been able to with the kitchen drinkers with whom he had to spend most of his time. Their conversation, from what he told me, had almost entirely to do with binges past and present, and sexual adventures that may have been true but probably weren't.

I suppose I could have asked him to tell me more about what had brought him to where he was—if he'd ever had a family, or a real job, but I mostly just sat watching him work. He painted with a terrific focus, an intensity I'd never seen in an adult before—there was something heroic about it, and I suppose he was the first real artist I'd ever met.

One afternoon—he was about halfway finished with his painting—as I got up to go into the kitchen, he told me he'd be leaving soon. By then I understood what that meant, that he'd gone longer than he could without drinking, and though I'd learned to sympathize, I still felt a little betrayed, not so much for myself, but because he hadn't finished the task he'd undertaken. I knew the owner would be doubly irritated with him, first because he'd have to go find another dishwasher, but more because now the station wagon had a partly painted sign and there wasn't likely to be anyone in the rural area where the camp was to finish it, and that now he'd speak of the painter with contempt—and I'd feel humiliated for him.

The next day he was gone, and remarkably enough, I had a postcard from him a few weeks later from the racetrack at Saratoga: there were only a few words on it, but they were written in a calligraphy as striking as the one he'd been using on the station wagon. I kept it for a long time; it may have been the first thing in my life I treasured just for its own sake, without having to authenticate its worth by sharing it with someone else. I wish I still had it.

Scents

Sweet to remember the tiny elevator I used to take to the garret someone had loaned me as an office and the way three people would crowd into its one-meter square and share our scents and stinks and emanations, even the half-thug from the floor below whose rock radio stations raged up through the ceiling at me but who must have spent half his pay on whatever cologne he soaked himself in, so raptly buoying it was.

And the woman who perfumed herself with something that threw me centuries back to some lost time of life I never lived but would passionately have liked to, and whom I suspect suspected by the way I inhaled her perfumes and powders and flesh scents, trying to keep them, keep them, that I was a clod and so manifested an edge of contempt in her glance at this pervert she was forced to slip past to get off.

And descending at lunchtime our rattling conveyance as patient as a donkey with two men from some Middle East country whose language I couldn't even name, how the rich reek of the meal they'd just eaten—onions and lamb—infused the minuscule volume of our shared air.

And once, outside on the sidewalk, a girl kissing her boyfriend goodbye, twice, thrice, who, as she swung before me, lifted the mass of her hair from her neck as though the day were terribly hot, which it wasn't at all, and I fancied the bouquets from that smooth nape trailing behind her like the cloud puffs from a skywriting airplane, so clear to me I felt if I walked a little higher on my toes, I could plunge my face in them and become a scented cloud myself.

Catherine's Laughter

Catherine

"How do you say it? Cat-ah-reen?"

"No, Cat-reen. And roll the *r* a little."

"Cat-ghreen?"

"Almost."

Her Laughter

There's no reserve, no hanging back in it, no thought of decorum, no thought of anything apparently except whatever has amused her or given her delight. It can also be splendidly . . . What? Hearty, raucous? No, those words are too coarse: her laughter always has something keen and sweet to it, an edge of something like song. It has volume, too, of course: in a group of people I can always hear her laughter soaring above everyone else's. Once, in a movie theater in New York, watching a French comedy much of the humor of which was lost in the subtitles, she laughed alone for almost the whole film, completely by herself, and never noticed.

When we first were together, I used to try to find a metaphor, a figure to specify what her laughter was like. What came closest was one of those funny, clunky wooden pull toys kids used to have, might still have for all I know—a duck, a too-long dachshund, a tiny elephant. I remember our son, Jed, had a bee, yellow and black with droll, resilient spring antennas and segmented legs.

Sometimes Jed would tug the bee behind him without bothering to look. The thing might not even be on its wheels anymore, it would just be bouncing helter-skelter, wonkety-wonk along, ricocheting onto its imperturbable nose, wobbling, rolling, bumping, snagging on cracks in the sidewalk, making brave little leaps like a salmon.

Like that her laughter was, and is, when something strikes her as funny, and she's already happy, which she almost always is—just like that, a toy a child is dragging unselfconsciously behind, just like that.

Crazy

Maybe it's just my age, but sometimes these days when I'm making love to Catherine it feels as though I'm really making love as much, or more—no, that's going too far, just as much—to her beauty. Is this unusual? Unhealthy? I have no idea. When I tell Catherine, she says she never thinks of herself as beautiful.

That's crazy, I say, you're fibbing.

No, she insists . . . Then, she admits, maybe once. When she was sixteen or so, in a resort town somewhere with her parents, she noticed people looking at her differently from the way they always had. She went back to her room and looked into the mirror, and she did indeed look beautiful to herself.

That's the only time, though.

Ha, I say: What about when O—— tried to kiss you? What about when M—— tried to hold your hand?

She laughs. Okay, maybe once or twice.

Ha. Once or twice. Ha.

Her Beauty

Men often find Catherine beautiful, and besides that the kind of beauty she has seems to make them feel free to tell her. "Beautiful," said a normally quite reserved, not to say quite often irascible sociologist friend when he met Catherine on the first walk she and I took when we came from Paris to Philadelphia. I introduced Catherine; he looked at her, shook her hand, and said it: "Beautiful." Just like that, not "She's beautiful," not "You're beautiful," just "Beautiful."

Which might seem odd, except it's precisely what a very unreserved poet, well known for his exuberance, said, too, also shaking her hand, when he met Catherine at one of his readings: "Beautiful."

Some other friends, too, a painter, another poet, same thing: "Beautiful," just like that, just that.

And I guess I should mention the famous man I won't name here who didn't say "Beautiful" when Catherine and I met him at a conference, but who, I found out from her after he died, had tried, unsuccessfully thank goodness, to convince her to come to his hotel room. I, as vigilant as I am—I really am, because I'm so fearfully jealous—suspected nothing, which I'm glad about now, because we came to cherish the man later as a friend, and it would have been difficult for me if I'd known.

The strangest thing is when I first met Catherine, I didn't think of her as all that beautiful. Nice-looking, certainly, pretty; but not really beautiful. I've often wondered why, but I can't remember, and I can't remember either when I did start thinking of her as beautiful. When we first met—it was at Kennedy Airport, our plane to Paris was ridiculously late—she was standing patiently in the line of passengers, and smiled in commiseration at me, I suppose already recognizing my pain-in-the-neck impatience. She was dressed, I remember perfectly, in a schleppy, shapeless black sweater, not very flattering jeans, and wore big eyeglasses. I smiled back but moved away because I was trying to find out what the hell was going on and the airline people were being very unhelpful.

After a few hours we were told the plane still hadn't arrived from Europe but that we'd be taken out to dinner. A bus came, I got on, and Catherine sat beside me. We didn't get to Paris for another day and a half, and by then we were friends, and soon after and ever since lovers.

Back to her beauty. I've been in quite a few situations when someone we don't know will look across a dinner table, say, and I'll realize that Catherine's beauty has suddenly dawned on them. There's always a slight look of surprise in their expression, almost shock, as though a light had been turned on around her. And that's just what it's like: when Catherine becomes interested in something, animated, involved in a conversation, an idea, an emotion, she takes on a kind of glow. I really can't explain it: she's just all at once beautiful, to me more beautiful.

I enjoy when that happens, when people—I purposefully don't say "men" because it happens with women, too—will fall in something like love with her. Sometimes, if the person is an attractive male, it doesn't make me terrifically happy. As I say, I'm painfully jealous, but I survive.

Faster

When the workmen came to unclog the cesspool of the tiny house in Greece Catherine and I had rented those first weeks we were together, they heaved the syrupy shit-gunk into the shallow cove in front of our terrace, and it settled through the vividly clear water into a gray layer on the rocks and pebbles at the bottom and stayed there.

The reason they did it was because the water that fed the house had been contaminated, but it was even more foul now—we couldn't drink it, cook, or even shower with it. There was a well, though, a little way up the hill behind us, and we'd walk there with a big ceramic jug to rinse ourselves off. The water was clean, but icy cold—I hated it.

Catherine appeared not to mind, but when I'd pour the water over her head and it would run down over her body, her skin would erupt in goose bumps—what a crude term for such a lovely phenomenon—and she'd all at once possess a different sort of corporality, solidity, depth.

"Breathtaking," another absurdly inadequate word, but my breath really would be taken—I'd gasp, my breathing would stop, then start again, faster, faster.

Talk

Catherine and I, for some long-forgotten reason, have both been irritable all day, touchy, pre-occupied, moody, and gloomy. Dinner is peaceful, though, and when we finish Catherine asks, "Are we going to make love tonight?"

I answer, "If I'm talking to you."

"You don't have to talk," Catherine says.

Dogs

When she walks our dog, Catherine tends to be a bit oblivious to how much mischief Bwindi might effect. She lets her wander at the end of her leash, even in the middle of town; sometimes the leash will get entangled around people's legs, and once Bwindi snatched a croissant out of the hand of a baby in a stroller. The baby howled, Catherine was very embarrassed and offered to buy another, but the amused mother declined.

When Catherine tells about that, she laughs, but recently there was a more dramatic incident. She was walking through the town near where we live when we're in France, and a woman, when she saw Bwindi approaching on her loose leash, stopped dead on the sidewalk, obviously frightened. Catherine noticed, brought Bwindi against her legs, and asked the woman what was wrong. The woman responded that she had a terror of dogs: she was Jewish, and when she was four, during the war, German soldiers came with police dogs and took away her parents and brother and sister and she never saw them again.

Hardly surprising she wouldn't care for dogs. She and Catherine chatted awhile and the woman told how she'd been saved when she'd been left alone in Paris, that she'd been sent to be brought up by a couple here in this town where she still lived.

Some years ago I saw a show in a museum of photographs of French people who had helped

Jews during the Nazi frenzy, taking them into their homes, hiding them, bringing them up as their own children. I wanted to write about it, but nothing I could say came close to doing justice to what was visible in the saved and saviors in those pictures: their simple, factual presences, no glow, no halos, nothing exalted in their expressions. They were real, as we all are, and that was enough.

In this case, though, it didn't turn out so well. The woman had been very unhappy with the couple who'd adopted her, and had had what sounded like a generally unfulfilling life.

Catherine was moved—that's not the way you want stories like that to end. But even the beginning . . . Catherine was only a few years younger than the woman; they'd both been born in Paris, perhaps blocks from each other. If Catherine had been a Jew . . .

There are matters that can't be coped with in reflecting on life, or love, or sometimes it seems anything at all.

Loobahsh

Catherine reads a lot, and quickly, and often listens to authors on the radio, both in France and in the States, then buys their books. Though very few turn out to be as interesting as their authors have made them sound, this doesn't deter her, she still listens, and buys, and reads.

When she brings a book to bed, as she always does before we go to sleep, she puts her feet up on the wall over the headboard. As she reads, one heel will rub lightly over the shin on her other leg, then go out straight so her legs are parallel again, lines ending in infinity, I think. Then the other leg will bend, move against the first, straighten out again and aim again.

Tonight, earlier in the evening we'd watched a DVD of a Hungarian movie, very stark, gloomy, about starving peasants, a father and daughter, and the peasants' broken-down, ill horse, and also, the last moments of the film implied, though you couldn't be certain, the end of the world. Much darkness, much raw fear.

There was very little dialogue, mostly single-word ejaculations the father and daughter passed between them and almost all of which were subtitled as "Fuck!" Their horse is dying: "Fuck!" Their well has run dry: "Fuck."

Later, Catherine in bed reading, me getting undressed, something falls clattering from her bedside table, Catherine mutters, "Fuck!" and I say, "That's what they said in the movie."

And Catherine, who didn't care for the film and watched only parts of it, says without looking up from her book, "Loobahsh."

"What?" I ask. "Is that the word?"

"Loobahsh," she says again, a grain of laughter in her voice.

"You made that up," I say to her. "Very funny."

Again, with a chuckle, "Loobahsh . . . Loobahsh."

Her left heel runs over her right shin, she flexes her foot then straightens her knee so her legs are parallel again, both aiming once more towards the planets and stars.

Oaks

After dinner, still at the table, I'm writing in my little notebook, scribbling fast, when Catherine says she'd like to take a walk. When I tell her I'm busy, she takes the empty dishes into the kitchen, then comes back.

"Come on, take a walk."

"I'm writing," I tell her.

"Take your notebook. You can take your wine, too."

"Wait just a minute," I say.

"You need a bigger notebook," Catherine says then. "I'll buy you a bigger notebook."

"I don't need a bigger notebook, and don't get me one."

"That's why I said it," Catherine says. "I just wanted to hear you say that. Let's go for a walk."

Finally I give up, give in, we stroll out across the park near our house and come to the pair of gigantic old oaks Catherine particularly loves. The trunk of each tree is about five feet across, and they stand close together, leaning a little as though making room for each other.

They're in full-leaved gorgeousness right now, and when we get to them Catherine says, "You have to come in here," and leads me between them.

"Now close your eyes," she says.

"Why?"

"Because there are all those branches above us," she answers, "and beneath us the roots. You have to listen."

I listen. "But I don't . . ." I start to object.

"You have to come stand here every day, then you will," Catherine answers, not laughing now. "You'll see, you will."

Codes

When the Rothschilds were accumulating their vast fortunes, and even after, they wrote their confidential business letters to other members of the family in code. Furthermore, these secret letters were not only written in the usual descending lines down the page, but the messages would also continue across the page in the other direction, making them essentially impossible for anyone not in the family to read.

How much of a factor the indecipherability of the letters actually was in the amassing of their empire, I have no idea, but I find it impossible not to think here of Robert Walser, the great Swiss author, writing, after he had gone insane, what are called now (though he never did) "microscripts," described by their translator as "narrow strips of paper covered with tiny, antlike markings ranging in height from one to two millimeters . . ." It was thought at first that they were nonsense, generated by the schizophrenia that had sent him to an asylum in 1929, where he would remain until his death, in 1956, but then they were deciphered. Some of them were written on the back of peoples' calling cards, some on the pages of tear-off calendars *which he'd cut in half* before he'd begin to write.

In a further complication, at some point he decided that pens had become his enemies, he could no longer trust them. Not daring to compose with them, he turned to less dangerous pencils, always very small ones. Painstakingly sharpened they must have been, those simple gadgets of graphite and wood, to be able to make such intricate inscriptions on those scraps as humble as the rags of desert saints.

I've always been struck by the raging commercial single-mindedness of the Rothschilds— but Walser, what passion, what devotion, and with writing tools that for all he knew were secret spies, secret foes.

They Call This

A young mother on a motor scooter stopped at a traffic light, her little son perched on the ledge between her legs, she in a gleaming helmet, he in a replica of it, smaller, but the same silvery color and just as shiny. His visor is swung shut, hers is open.

As I pull up beside them on my bike, the mother is leaning over to embrace the child, whispering something to him, and I'm shaken, truly shaken, by the wish, the need, to have those slim, strong arms contain me in their sanctuary of affection.

Though they call this regression, that implies a return to some past state, and this has never left me, this fundamental pang of being too soon torn from conditions of bliss that promise ever more bliss, no matter that the scooter's fenders are pimpled with dents, nor that as it waits, it pops impatiently, clears its throat, growls.

A Jew, a Road, Some Crows

"I am dying of the itch," he thinks; a wheel jolts in a rut, the plank seat slaps at him, "or of this wretched cart," he thinks, kicking the mare's gaunt haunch, "or of the stink. Father in heaven, cure me of my wretched stink, cure me of my itch, cure me, Father, of whatever next affliction you have stored up in your stinking palace of a hell for me."

Fallow fields, a road that winds out listlessly ahead, pricking the horizon, vanishing; east and west stripped winter trees, lowering clouds, a frozen river; crows.

"Who has called me back," he thinks, "who has brought me back to toil along this road, to watch these crows that wait for me to die so they can eat the eyes I loathe them with? Who would bring me back through these erasures and annihilations, my oblivion, my sleep? Once I slept, now I can't remember if I peddled rags or grain or air, or if I starved or ate."

A village, oiled paper windowed huts, roofs leaking rain, doors leaking wind; a dark that spreads like thickening oil over the bitter snow; the cold, the crows.

"Whoever called me back, let me go again. What meaning can I have for you? Do you mean to mourn? Who? Me? Yourself? Am I the one who'll let you mourn your dissipating history, your self thinned out of all but mythlessness and waste? Am I to be your lens? What other meaning will I have, peddling wheat or rags or gold?"

Konskiwolie, Mazelbożec, Korznice, Glisk. Between them fallow fields, rutted roads, bitter cold. A Jew, a road, some crows.

Friendship

Some days the best thing in a museum isn't the art, the paintings or statues, even those, say, from ancient Greece—a frieze of women, their dresses pouring like water—but maybe because you're depressed, or distracted, or too something anyway to be anything but hopeless about human aspiration and hope, it's rather the people who are there with you, the schoolchildren earnestly measuring and sketching, the young couple embracing—he loves her but she loves, you can tell, her new dress, as soon as he lets her go she runs her hands down the panels of its shining fabric again—even the woman who talks too loudly to her husband in some indecipherable language and who when the guard tries to shush her beams brightly back at him as though he'd said something amusing, and the rather rough-looking guy who's obviously been dragged here by his wife, a plump, pleasant-looking woman. He plops down on a bench, loudly sighs, then makes believe he's collapsing of exhaustion, ending up horizontal, staring wide-eyed at the ceiling as though he were dead.

Right past him I notice a relief, Greek, too, that I've never looked at closely. Two men with shields, their bodies at first apparently at ease, shaking hands; then I notice one is doing so a bit more insistently than the other, his hand more forcefully, rigidly extended. The other is merely allowing his hand to be taken—his slight tilt away and the slouch of his shoulders indicate reluctance, or suspicion—perhaps he's been offended and if this is an apology, he doesn't want to let his having been offended go, or not completely, not yet.

"His having been offended . . ." Peculiar to think so many centuries after.

The lazy husband and his wife are gone, so are the lovers. Just me, and the guard, defending those once-fleeting emotions in stone.

Sybil

What must I do, to her, to myself, to believe or imagine I can believe in her? Ocher hills, I think, pale, dusty low green shrubs of wild thyme; darker cypresses, "cemetery trees" they're called these days; then squat clay or stacked stone houses, a cave, a crypt, with off to the side a priest or suppliant asleep on the still blood-soaked skin of a slaughtered sheep or goat.

Then I see, across a hillside, something moving, taking up some small portion of my field of vision—does my anticipation make it seem to take up more? When my eyes focus on it, yes, perhaps, but when I look away, it seems precisely what it should be, in scale and density. Is it she? How know?

What's more apprehensible is what I smell: a stink, a stench, like something I sniffed once in an unswept, unwatered cage of starving bears; or in the plastic container I opened by mistake with months-old chunks of seething rotted meat inside it: the way my head snapped back without my meaning it to. All that, mingled with never-washed secret female flesh; soured menstrual emissions, rotted teeth, scab and self-inflicted filth.

And what could she possibly look like? I'm stuck with such trite imagery—madwoman from a play, wild woman from a film; disheveled mane, rags of burlap, feet and ankles bound in tattering strips like compresses on running wounds.

And then she speaks: whispered hiccupings of disconnected consonants, like someone choking on food, someone else's throat funneled down by illness. And what she finally says: the cadence is wrong, the lilt, the violence of voice with which she's afflicted won't allow for de-encrypting.

No language music—I know enough to know there'd be none of that: a grunt instead, a cry of rage.

Do I yet believe in her? Do I remember why I came to her, and what I meant to ask? What I meant to know?

Sixty

When I offhandedly remarked to my father how sad it was that his good friend Sol would be dying next year he startled and asked what do you mean and I answered well he'll be sixty won't he so he'll die and my father said what are you talking about and I said well when you're sixty that's when you die everybody knows that and then my father "disabused" me—is that the term?—of that notion which it turns out was true for the men on the island—Kea—where the poet Simonides came from because when they hit sixty all the males drank hemlock and removed themselves got out of the way you might put it which doesn't seem like that bad an idea when I wake creaking and crackling and drag myself out of my sleep and also sometimes just seeing something like that half-fossilized woman yesterday in the street old old with a too-short skirt—"mini" are they still called?—bright tights high leather boots thick makeup head shaved and one long earring dangling and my god what's she thinking I thought then glimpsed in my mind what pleasure for her it must have been to put her face on choose the outfit unroll the tights don the sweater hook on the earring then *hup* out the door and I remembered also what it was for myself this morning when I was shaving number sixty long gone old yellow teeth like teeth in a skull then I saw in the glass indeed a skull my skull orbs dead as moons cracked grin leering and how could I have let myself get so old I thought I must not have paid enough attention I must have left too many days only partly put to use otherwise it would have taken longer to get here longer so much longer

Again

One of my grandsons is running through the park towards me to show me something he's found—a long white feather—I can see it from here—probably from one of the herons that come at dawn to fish in the pond.

It doesn't matter which grandson it is: in my memory, it could be one, or another, or all—I'd prefer it were all, each in his brilliant singularity, each in his union with the rest.

There's a broad plane tree between us, and for some reason my grandson as he runs keeps moving left and then right, so he disappears behind the trunk of the tree, appears again, disappears, appears, vivid in the brilliant sunlight, again is gone, again is there, all the while beaming with pride at bearing such treasure to share with me.

Also he calls my name each time he appears, and as I stand waiting, listening, watching him materialize again, it comes to me that if that old legend of having your life flash before you as you die is true, I'll have this all again, and again.

New
Poems

(2015)

The Sun, the Saint, the Sot

1.

Oh, sun, bright star, *our* star, dearest, nearest, how solacing you remain, how consoling your illuminations,

what relief on a day in our epoch of dire planet anguish to have you flinging your reliable light.

Oh, cosmological fast-baller, underwhelming only to the demented, like that saint who conceived you

"groaning for deliverance," which he promised in the end you'd "trade your shining carapace for."

Deliverance? Carapace? Sun, can you hear my teeth grinding? Can you hear my dried-out battered brain,

my already broken down thought-thing rattling like a bean in a gourd down a hill in a hailstorm?

It's because they're still here around us, the soul-gobblers! The god-slobbering carapace-snatchers

who stalk from their altars to government chambers to blight what's left of our earthly adventure.

Wrenching, no, shameful, no, hideous, frightening, to admit I, too, once yearned to "believe" as they do,

because I desired, craved, the *peace* Buddha and Blake and innocent Gospel Thomas kept humming about,

because I wished *rapture* as much as the tits, thighs, and asses that obsessed me then in truth
　　more,
as now the future, the inferno-doom of our darling earth's future, obsesses me more even than
　　that.

Oh, future, oh, earth-orphan, that you, irresistible gleamer, cunningly coaxed into your orbit—
our world in its robes of azure and lace is dimming, we have to behold its darkening de-
　　nouements,

and where are the bibles to buoy me? Where are the Vedas, the *I Ching*s, the shamanic ravings
whose useless pages I stuffed myself with in the abyss of my intellectual-spiritual uncoming-
　　of-age?

　　2.

Back in the story what happens next I'm sure you'll recall, all-beholder: *philosophy* finds me,
philosophy with a swirl of its logical cape and its chariot of gilded conceptual calves comes
　　to me

in the form of that teacher in college with lamentable teeth the same alarming beige hue as
　　his toupee
who gazed out the window as he lectured and sometimes would drift to a stop and smile to
　　himself,

because, he finally admitted, he was *content* because he was a follower of *Berkeley* and *Kant*
　　and their ilk,
who'd conclusively proved that "only mind and its mental objects exist . . ." and *Yes*, I thought,

yes, that's the answer I need, because weren't they saying that *nothing was real except in my psyche?*
Even you, sun, were a match-flare, nothing actual was true, and if I wanted to I could make it all stop,

as now I find myself telling it all to *Just stop*, I find myself pleading, *Just all go away, go away,*
the glaciers melting, the tundra turning to methane, the oceans rotting to scum—blot them, erase them.

But here's my professor again and here am I noting that more often than not in class he was tipsy,
and the rumor that he spent his weekends self-exiled on skid row must have been tragically true,

so how could I not understand that this was where such epistemological hijinks would lead me—
to drink hemlock and lie down with the nameless and shameless and hope again it would all go away . . .

Thus were you saved, mighty unflincher, and now, as craven as we are before our wounded world, save us—
let us linger in your lethal warmth, don't scant our meager spinnings in the great celestial waltz.

Bark

Big dog bark not big dog just big bark I know him up our street
little dog in electric fence startles me when my own dog and I pass
Watch out! minuscule mutt with mighty voice bark-shouts *Listen up!*

And such truly big barks after all . . . like . . . ? Death's first to mind
death too much these days on my mind I tell myself bark at myself
how not with big dog death not up the road but here in my breast

my bone marrow my blood cells' indecipherably syllabled names
scrabbling and snarling behind their own invisible fences
like the fears I hardly hear anymore so incessant their barkings

and isn't it worse nearly that death can seem a friendly old dog
ready to save you if you call it that from the little dog roaring
of everything else doesn't everything else bark more often than death

even louder sometimes so come to me death barks don't flee me
but which fear you flee won't matter to those big dog or small
fierce fusses on your street or inside you listen or not there they are

Soul in Steel

You would have said that they were men of iron . . . they had
head accouterments so neatly fitted . . . M O N T A I G N E

1.

Not frail not fainthearted flighty and I certainly don't mean merely to mean unmale with those
   now
happily unacceptable connotations of frivolous faithless flirty emphatically no innuendo like
   that
I mean rather shouldn't I be able to conceive a yes unmale soul for this bundle of matter and
   pain
with qualities that might seem feminine fragile but that would enlarge instead of diminish me?

2.

Some other soul-something that might one day contain all of life I've omitted because my manly
I have to admit my all too often martial militaristic soul-machine with its invariably impatient
enraged enraging responses squats boiling in my cockpit like a senator calling again for more
   war
enacting those testosterone rituals that finish always in slashes and snarls and the will to
   prevail

3.

Prevail prevail I glare at you through my eyeholes I snort through the rifled slits of my
   nostrils

the fumes of your terror (or is it my own?) my brain solder hardens in the aching shells of my
   ears
so I can't hear myself begging for pity can't hear myself beseeching not to be slaughtered as
   I've been
in every one of my soul-lives every one of my tales and legends every lamentable re-existing
   in history

   4.

Where does it come from this prevailing whence arises this ravenousness for victory for
   triumph
must I wait hopelessly as my timorous untested soul tries to emerge in me like a newborn and
   survive
when I revert again when I'm fighter again hero again warrior king helplessly once more who
   I am
waving my spear manifesting my soul of steel screwed down in gestures of rage and reflexive
   revenge?

   5.

Reconceived soul terrified of the ever violent world what shall I comfort her with what shall
   I sing her
Oh beauty beauty my love sighed when a doe materialized to gaze at us from the marge of a
   wood
Oh beauty beauty wouldn't that be enough not Persephone Eve or Helen not even Anna or
   Molly
just the voice that rises without your willing it to and breathes beauty beauty wouldn't that be
   enough?

The World and Hokusai

Like a little boy with his daddy world takes Hokusai's hand to be led through the wilds of doubt
and derision yes even derision because so many crybabies keep yowling *Stop, World! You hurt!*
but Hokusai with all his bequeathments keeps on and poor put-upon world sighs with relief

because here's Hokusai's elephant thirty feet tall with tiny bald either elf-creatures or angels
or maybe who knows even regular humans in striped pants and smocks trying to scale it
to figure out what it could possibly be but isn't it clear that Hokusai's elephant has to be *world*?

Look how it winks from the side of its wise patient eye and the shelves of skin hanging
    across it!
No actual elephant ever had so many Fuji wrinkles and cracks—it has to be Hokusai's world
and who else could cook up an elephant-world but him? The rest of us find just living so hard

we have to convince ourselves not to give it all up, and do what? . . . Take naps? Write a book?
Anyway here's Hokusai!—yay!—pen sharp as a dart and Look he proclaims I've drawn a
    soldier
firing a crazy cannon who knows why into some waves The smoke! The turmoil! The tumult!

But note also please how the soldier is smiling looking just fine indifferent unconcerned bland
and old Hokusai must have been smiling too into his fist elephants cannons really after all
what excruciations could afflict someone who'd sign work "Seen with the eyes of a blind man"?

But what if he ever gets tired of dragging petulant world behind him what if he closes up shop
who'd keep it going? Not me I'm just an old word-spider slung here scritch-scratching the
    keys—
Hokusai would be laughing but where would I find an elephant where would I come up with
    a world?

Hog

In a certain town in New Jersey where now will be found malls car dealerships drive-throughs
highways with synchronized lights a motor vehicle office a store selling discount something or
    other
I can't remember what else but haven't we all experienced such post-agrarian transmogri-
    fications

In a certain town in New Jersey once was a farm farmed by a Jewish farmer a *Jewish farmer*
my goodness a notion I'd never entertained Jews were lawyers accountants doctors maybe
    salesmen
until a friend took me to meet one his uncle his mother's brother who lived somewhere I'd
    never heard of

In a certain town in New Jersey not far from where I am now existed a farmer who was also a
    Jew
who'd eluded the second war murders by leaving for the States with nothing in his wallet or
    satchel
but a hammer and saw and a handful of nails and worked his way through the shit-pit of Europe
    to here

where he went back with somebody else's money some earlier escapee-arrival's maybe his
    sister's
to farming which had been his family's trade for many generations in the old country he boasted
and there he was on his farm now with his chickens and corn and I saw three or four cows and
    some pigs

and on this day a dead hog that is to say a hog he'd only just slaughtered that hung upside
    down

from a hook in a rafter and a stout iron chain and which the farmer the Jewish farmer was
    flinging

boiling water against flinging and flinging so its bristles would soften which I could see they
    had

for then he was scraping the hog with a crescent-shaped length of steel and the bristles were
    loosening

and I gathered that when they were gone he'd be (how had the word ever found me) *gutting*
    the hog

there was a gleaming well-honed knife at the ready whose task I could tell was slicing you
    open

as you horribly swung there colorless gunk spooling out of your snout while the booted farmer

methodically effected the everlasting labor of farmers Jewish or not pulling you with his knotty
    arms

and leather gloves towards him to cut you apart and sell you I supposed is what would come
    next

In a certain town in New Jersey might anyone remain to ask forgiveness for the concrete and
    asphalt

the forests felled for McMansions the eternally lost corn and wheat fields and vanished
    orchards

might anyone recall the sweet stink of manure of tilled earth the odor even of fresh blood on
    a floor

and who besides me will remember the farmer so imposing in the masterful exercise of his
    calling

who with a snort and a clap on the back forgave me the gawk of my adolescence as imagining

the rest of what life would be bringing I knelt by a rusting soon to be scrapped hay rake and
    threw up

I Emerge from the News

Not like a polar bear erupting from the water beside the edge of his glacier because as we
    know glacier and bear are on the path to extinction and extinct things never emerge they
    subside they sink they bubble away in the warm-as-blood poisonous foam

It can't either be like dolphin tiger otter homo-sapien homo-destructus for all are mere phases
    in the fleeting conglomerations of matter as expressed by let me think who would that be
    some Gnostic dreamer some Kabbalist nut job?

    *

I try with great exertion to extract myself this day or perhaps it was yesterday I can't remember
    from my usual dose of the news from which I have so far in these few hours already ingested
    many urgent not to say crucial items of information local national planet-wide but which I
    deign to regurgitate here

for I was speaking of emerging not drowning of escaping not being attacked again slaughtered
    and dissected by these horrid revealments

    *

This was the day I had thought I'd attempt to keep track of the dead in the news each individual
    death that arrived from the news from each and every war assassination terror attack gov-
    ernment torture of dissidents simple murder etc

but it took a mere moment to realize the task was impossible the individual deaths were clog-
    ging the circuits of my brain like indigestible particles in a drainpipe and I had to release
    them let them flow again in their roaring unstoppable excremental gush

*

Perhaps though one day I will escape from my obsessive engrossments with the news as I hope and will I emerge then like a tulip from its bulb to wave my shy petals in gentle medieval zephyrs?

Or will I screech and shriek as I did I can almost remember when I wished to escape as a child from my imprisoning crib those relentless bars I peered through already a prisoner in the world of events beyond me?

*

But perhaps I will never emerge for even today despite all my efforts and denials my emergence is partial

I remain a newly metamorphosed moth its cocoon snagged on a twig the blasting sun already parching my sensitive thorax

Or a bridge worker a rung of whose ladder has given way leaving him suspended in a realm where the world of breath and the world of non-breath are no longer distinguishable by his paralyzed hope

Or a priest pope rabbi shaman whose death lifts him out of his gold figured robe his healthy scarlet complexion defiantly shining

*

But stop perhaps it's time to consider whether the news at the end disadheres from consciousness and conscience easily with a slight almost gratifying twinge like a surgical scab?

If so why not pry up a corner and tear it off quickly for aren't the elements of the news always
scabs of some newly ancient affliction?

Or does the news obdurately cohere does it glue itself nail itself solder itself to the most deeply
seated neurons in our chains of awareness and does with them arrive always anxiety an-
guish a sense of the inevitably inescapable?

  *

But at last here is the moment I've waited so long for when I will have emerged and achieved
partial oblivion and at least for a moment or minute am free

The blessed instant when the newspaper has fallen from my hand to the floor beside me and
I have not yet turned on the coverage which ignites the telly with its regurgitations twenty-
four on twenty-four constantly and forever

The moment

Brilliant

  *

News news though you're back as I knew you'd be to take me to you to hold me as you plunge
me through channel two channel two million

But soon I'll escape again I know it how can I not?

This time though when you finish with me will you allow me to flee your clutches like a soft-
bodied crab skittering back into the tide of history and death?

Or must I eternally convulse in your armored unfeeling claw?

Polar bear glacier beautiful skittering crab of the human soul

Please allow me to continue to emerge

Not again to subside

*

Please permit me also a last moment of causeless reflection

Don't leave me here staring longingly towards the television as though towards a sky I can no
longer see as I can no longer see the broken glass of existence shattering upon us

Allow me to emerge

Not to subside into the sludge we suspect boils at the root of the tree of our life

Our life

which was our life

Little Hymn to Time

Da Da Freud, Ma Ma Marx, growly Uncle Sartre—what a theory zoo to do your adoles-
   cence in.
Everything'd been figured out, dialectic existential ego schemes—such fun, but then, oh my,
reality arrives—the sergeant at the draft board roaring if we ran away they'd drag us back in
   chains . . .

I was ready to desert before I had my gun—it hardly mattered, though, they didn't need us
   then,
there wasn't any war: horrid Heil Hitler you were dead; stinky Stalin in your bloody tunic, too:
no war, no chains, I'd wriggled free, and there was all this wild new music—what to do but
   dance?

Even after Cuba came, and 'Nam, and no more wriggling free, you could dim your brain with
   pot,
break your brain with acid, and if you hadn't you could make believe you had, so still could
   dance,
and, this was splendid, better, best, could fuck yourself and any friendly body you could find
   to bliss.

Chant to me of ba ba bliss, choir to me your fee-fi-fo of fucking, your merry-go-round of
   disheveled beds.
What matter if the world wasn't as we thought it would be cured of everything but love and
   bliss?
What matter just so long as we could dance and fuck—who in half a century will care if we
   were wrong?

Dance away the years, we thought, leave the dream behind, but isn't it still in you, isn't it still
   you?

I close my eyes and there we are again—I can hear the music but who knows what any of it meant?

Gone the dancing, gone the bliss, just those errors and illusions that stud our ancient hearts like nails.

Smashed Nail

As though the stone was skin on a blossom of air a gathering of breath
As though it had carved itself from the names it had been given
And weighed less than the emperors kings goddesses it embodied

Isn't it this we sense beholding our great fortresses pyramids temples
That the stones the mighty stones had a life of their own planet-pieces
Balancing themselves on their underparts linking each to the next

There were no builders there we intuit no masters masons slaves
Who would need masters or slaves when the stones carved themselves
Who would need slaves for this or anything else in the world of matter?

Would it not be a waste of intellect to characterize humans as *slaves*
And treat them as such in Mesopotamia Athens Charleston Accra
Other outposts where slaves were *"the principal source of mercantile wealth"*

All this I thought as after my hammer smashed my nail it turned blue
pyramids temples gods I thought as my traitor nail throbbed to itself
As I imagined some ancestor stone lifted itself one day but forgot itself

Trembled free and alit crashing on some slave ancestor's finger and
Ai ai the whole system of slavery isn't worth this ai smashed nail
Ai the whole cruel history of humanity comes down floating smashing

Down on some biblical town everything slaughtered but the slaves
Slaves have worth unlike the husbands wives children to be ground
In the mill wheel of vengeance keep the slaves they're worth something

Even with throbbing blue fingers can't they plow cook clean even screw
Didn't some of them sing some act as surrogate husbands and wives
Even after they broke their backs in mines their legs in quarries their fingers

Smashed nail what art thou to me throbbing at the end of my mortal flesh
Ancestor slave were you loved sister slave were you admired brother slave
Are you still with me as we quarry the stone fit it drop it forever in place?

Tears

Baby next door crying, not angry crying or sad, *hungry* crying—*feed me, feed me, feed me* crying.
Now Mama must do it, baby stops crying—sweet to think of her at filling station of bottle or breast.

Not sweet my own crying-not-crying, not hungry or angry these tears that keep rising then stopping,
tremblingly shimmering higher inside me than ever but never spilling, never releasing—

this silent sob, this unuttered wail, this dolorous weeping for our *our* that sends its bitterest burning
from my conscience to its fountain of tears to the arid well of my eyes with their taps ever shut.

Our *our*, meaning *our land, our oceans, our sky, our trees, animals, insects*—who else's are they?—
and our children, their children, our friends' and enemies' children's children—our our and our all.

Baby starts in again, crying again, stopping and starting, trying like us to *mean* surely something,
prove surely something, the way we, ruiners, wasters, try to prove again we're right, always *right*,

in all things, so that we won't cry ourselves empty, our mental husks blown away as in a storm,
though we've so muddled our actual storms they hardly know which way to blow or how howl.

Shouldn't we, too, ask, *How howl?* Not: *Nourish us, earth, unbeloved, please, again and forever.*
Too late for that—too late even for *please*—please stay, please endure—too late for everything,
   all.

Silence again, baby must be asleep—consoling to think of lifting again that ever unlikely
   lightness,
not though to hear once more those unwhispered whispers, those unpled pleas—*Hold me,*
   Hold me . . .

The Prick

1.

Don't make me tell it who's making me tell it why in the name of anything tell anything at all

and while I'm at it why "it" for the singular won't do "it" would have to be "them" or even "all"

have to be every single offense every sin every affront every insult omission and ethical lapse

all piled together in a swarming stack like manure in the yard after a thaw alive with white worms

White worms is me swarming is me the stink of shit putrescence of dead things at the heart of the heap

is me too as much as I was in bed with this girl and that making promises I didn't even know were

then white worm and swarm white worm that creeps out of the muck of memory I'd see one or another

years later and they'd look at me with such loathing that I realized I hadn't known what "loathing"

meant nor "hatred" nor "despicable" "vile" and I'd forgotten all about them and which was worse

forgetting them then or knowing now I'll never have the chance to ask them to forgive me *Forgive me*

2.

There I've told it maybe not the whole thing but the whole thing would be such a long twisted list

I flee from myself continually such a saddening list I hardly recall half the crap-headed things

I managed to accomplish not to speak of all the much more urgent matters I left out or deleted

not the white worms nor the breasts of that girl so young now I plotted so hard to hold in my hands

and inhale it seems everything then was there to inhale to ingest to capture to hang on to and hoard

as the past now is hoarded though the prick knows how can he not that the memories are fading

or isn't this worse the good memories are fading the prick memories hang on and claw and dig in

resist and insist and who knows if at the end it may be that nothing will be left but those compilations

those collections of dung-diddle that should have been cut should have been left on the editing floor

but here he is prick of the earth wound in those celluloid strips each worth a moment each costing

a mountain each with some inexpugnable accusation and what he can do now the reprehen-sible prick

but whine and call out for help as though anyone else could save him or he might save himself?

At What Time on the Sabbath Do Vultures Awake?

Yesterday at four in the afternoon there were as accurately as I could count sixteen on fence
    posts

and branches banking or dive-bombing might be the better term down towards a dead deer in
    a gulley

but this morning at dawn there were none none at all as I trekked by so I thought they'd
    consumed

the corpse or emptied its guts but no there it still was though I didn't come too close for the
    stench

then later on my way back were first five then at least a half dozen more circling over their
    quarry

a few scrolling down towards it and how not wonder whether they'd overslept or if on Sundays

like this they just like to lie around reading the paper not bothering to get up till day's going

full blast and the great pouring clouds of chattering starlings are already in flight heading
    south

or maybe it's not till they're stiff from too many hours in their nests or when they feel their
    rectums

contract in anticipation of the feast surely still stewing out there in the high browning weeds

that they unfold their elaborate wings and their crampy prosthetical legs stretch their hideous
    necks

and hurl themselves into the waiting air which to them must be a syrupy upsoaring netting

and then as the light in the dearest distance brightens and moves down over the hillsides
    bedazzled

with late autumn hues and the new winter chill becomes something you can almost ingest they clamber onto the carcass to drive the blunt blades of their beaks into the well-softened flesh

fully awake now and how be otherwise on a day portending such glorious craving and fulfillment?

Beethoven Invents the Species Again

FOR RICHARD GOODE

1.

As is the case every day though we don't always know it here we are waiting for Beethoven
to kick-start the species again get us going on being wholly human again we're anxious
    about it
as usual existence as usual driving us to distraction we muttering hatchlings fragmented

just as we were when we were half-beings before music found us it took so long for music to
    find us
remember? back when we'd taught ourselves only to chip carve hammer spear points or blades
while our psyches stricken with longing kept burbling up blurred intimations of *more* we
    mixtures

condemned to inhabit recalcitrant realms where tree was tree hill hill earth soil lake etcetera
all *thing*-things entrenched in stony obstinate factness though we kept wanting more than fact
more even than what we could brain-glue together centaur minotaur harpy please more more

we cried always in pieces hoping for what we still couldn't speak as again we hoisted our
    hatchets
but wait someone said wait Beethoven still says says again always what of sound world-sound
    or wind
wolf-sound or water might the way be in listening rather than making or thinking even or
    praying?

2.

Not only Beethoven still says Mozart also and Bach and Schubert Chopin Ella and Woody and
    Miles

and the rest we can trace all of them back because somewhere in us we still hear that first hol-
    low pipe

in a cave then Hermes devising the lyre and Orpheus tuning it up and before you know it harp
    fiddle

and piano! bravo! finally Beethoven's piano listen again how the notes knit together then the
    chords

how the melodies climb the beckoning rows of their scales and we're lifted once more to
    coherence

we and that ravenous void in us brought together for this shining time as music again fashions

the hallowed place where our doubts and frailties are lathed like dross from our ancient
    confusions

and where as we attend we're no longer half-things we once-collages we're whole who couldn't
    tell

if we were hawks humans horses we're complete now not hanging out of the scabbard of
    matter

but caught by contained and spun from the music that embodies those ever unlikely con-
    nections

while in our rapture at being transformed again into musical selves a note a chord at a time
    we exist

as we knew all along thank you Beethoven thank you the rest we should have and now once
    again do

I Shot a Frog I Shot a Bird

I shot a frog

It had been squatting apparently waiting for something
perhaps the end of the world I thought from its obstinate stillness
on a rock at the edge of a tiny pond
I'd say no more than a yard edge to edge

The frog was small too not one of those big bulls
that lurk in the reeds by a lake who can scare you
so solemn they are so sure of themselves their fat selves
with their down-turned mouths
and great oinks

I shot the frog
the very small frog
with a Winchester .22 caliber rifle
because there was nothing else to shoot there right then
or nothing but an inanimate target and how boring that had become
meaningless thwacks into wood
once or twice splinters and the thing was half blasted apart
so
so what?

Then there was the frog and my rifle lifted itself as though by itself
aimed as though by itself
fired as though by itself
and the frog

well

the frog vanished
not even a splash or sprinkle of blood
not even a cloud of blur the way computers do it these days for films
just gone disappeared vanished kaput

frog
no frog

I wasn't pleased
this was not as I'd planned it

I'd shot the frog
because I wanted to shoot the rifle again
someone had loaned me to amuse myself with

I'd already felt the subtle painless jolt in my shoulder each time it went off
that very benign but definite crack
in more than your ear

you sense it in the drum of your chest in the tangle even of your groin
nothing like pain
nothing really like pain
but a definite crack a definite

jolt

　　*

I shot a bird

This was another year though the same rifle
the same person letting me use it

He was sick in bed nothing serious a slight fever
he just couldn't go out
I remember there was nothing to do
so we took the rifle out of the closet
and a bunch of those inconsequential-appearing bullets
hardly half an inch long
and shot out the window first at a paper target I stuck on a tree
but that was boring

then he had a model plane he'd made as a kid
hanging from his ceiling of his bedroom
and I suggested what about that and he said
why not he was over that kid stuff

so I hung the plane some war plane a Messerschmitt maybe
from a branch in the tree and we were going to take turns
but on my first shot my bullet blew it apart
nothing was left but a string swaying
nothing to shoot but the string and who shoots at string?

Then a sparrow I think or a lark I can't bring it back quite
so long ago was it I only picture some common sparrow or lark
flittering down to the branch next to the one
the plane had hung from

and my rifle still in my arms
as they will as I've mentioned they will
lifted itself
aimed itself
for I had such incompetent aim
my hands would tremble
the sight thing on the rifle's far end would swing
back and forth and almost always I'd miss
except with that frog

And now this bird

Foolish thing to have stopped there right then
foolish thing to land there and stay there how long
half an instant on that branch
and the gun went off as they will and the jolt jolted my shoulder
and the bird fell

It didn't vanish though as had the frog
it didn't take itself out of the world
it just had no head any longer
it lay on the ground whole but headless

Do you believe me?
There was no head on that bird
only a body headless therefore frightening therefore repulsive

Broken clump in the dirt wings tucked into its body as though it still lived
flightless and broken in the dirt
almost the same color as dirt

Or so I remember
I'm not making it up
I swear everything else here is true
so why would I make up a bird?

Haven't I proved
I aimed a gun
shot a gun
had fun with a gun?

Had fun with a gun
with a gun?

The Economy Rescued by
My Mother Returning to Shop

I sleep as always these dark days aquiver I awake atremble my limbs jerk I thrash like a gaffed
   shark

no not shark too many sharks already fiscal financial that's why gullible guppy I was I thought

the boom wouldn't bust the bubble not burst shred leave us hanging over this thorny dollarless
   void

Markets staggered sales down the chute confidence off the cliff the aisles of the box stores and
   chains

depeopled ghost towns even the parking lots empty the lane lines in martial formation like
   wings

stripped of their feathers forlornly signaling for interstellar relief how not quiver not jerk and
   thrash?

Wait don't give up too soon here comes my mother back from beyond and she's going to shop!

Avid sharp-eyed alert gleaming and beaming as she always was on our old bus expeditions
   downtown

with a vigilance keen and serene and hands entities sentient and shrewd cunningly separate
   from her

evolved to analyze things intrinsic or better overlooked worth as they collate the goods on their
   racks—

a blouse in silk and on sale!—which she shows an admiring mirror and opens her wallet and
   buys

buys as that president told us we should though only my mother has sufficient passion to effect
   this

Didn't I once watch her unwrap a pair of new shoes to inhale the scent of their unblemished
   soles
and in the very next quarter didn't the GNP begin to stir the number of long-term unemployed
   slip
because of my mother's single-minded devotion to the subtlest aspects of commerce and
   exchange?

And all this after growing up poor in my grandmother's half-starving canned-green-pea
   kitchen
and after surviving Depression and War how did she garner so much abstruse lore on
   redistribution
how accrue so many practical speculations about what we'd need to correct these failures and
   flops?

Delighted the gods of money must be to behold her again as she conveys herself through their
   portals
Here's ingenious Hephaestus devising for our enchantment his gadgets and gizmos and
   glitter
and here Hermes publicity marketing sales (not Hermès shrine for the rich and pretend rich)

and vast Hades who lurks in the fear beneath all waiting to drag us down to the realm of dire
   want
where a hound with three heads a banker's a hedge funder's an under-prime mortgage
   broker's
snarls as my mother who once filched from her sister coins she didn't have to buy me an ice
   cream

croons as she crooned then Make it last and retires to her couch and opens her credit-card
   statement

and pays isn't it splendid to be able to pay for your new skirt your sheer stockings your eau
de toilette

and so redeem the Dow and the Nasdaq and hallow us all for our humble hungers our almost
innocent greed?

Mantis

1.

What in the name of anything on earth was I doing crawling behind a billboard next to a
  bakery
a few blocks from the grammar school I attended then which recently made it into the news
because drug dealers killed some teenagers there three boys and a girl making them kneel by
  a wall
I realized must be the one in the field where we used to have gym class and gunning them
  down

2.

Beneath the billboard seethed eons of trash rotted food shit human or dog who knows what
  else
except I knew what else as soon as I saw it a praying mantis four five maybe more inches long
on a swaying weed not a foot from my face an appalling contrivance I'd never seen even a pic-
  ture of
but with its swiveling ball-bearing head and opaque expressionless eyes I knew wanted to
  harm me

3.

Gunning them down What would our kindly teachers hands white with chalk dust have
  thought?

Our violence was games like dodge ball or its other name when we played it inside *bombardment*

the bigger kids blasting balls off the backs of the smaller with much groaning and feigned cries of pain

Gunning them down the mind skids from reason to cause cause to reason but nothing coheres

4.

The female mantis bites the head off then devours its male after they couple which means *fuck*

I guessed when I looked up in *The Book of Knowledge* the monster with which I'd had my run-in

Though the text claimed they were harmless I still believed the malevolent creature gazing at me

those fore-claws barbed like a lumberjack's saw had been gathering the rest of itself to attack

5.

What's there now I wonder would the bakery still be and the billboard though what was a billboard

doing anyway at the very edge of our city what would it have been hawking soap cigarettes cars?

In memory those were the days before everything was for sale before buying and selling became all

but maybe I'm wrong maybe I just don't remember there's so much I've managed not to remember

6.

I haven't seen a mantis for a long time but if I met one I wouldn't be frightened of it but *for* it
so fragile they look so brittle their ill-fitting parts fastened together like biplanes from the first
   world war
When I'd escaped mine that day I headed home taking as you still could in those pre-heroin
   years
a shortcut through the school yard where kids were playing hide-and-seek behind that same
   wall

Dear Reader

Dear reader dearest inscrutable listener inscrutably harking or regrettably more likely not
   harking
except in that chamber in me that posits you with me every moment I'm speaking or trying to
   speak

Dear reader who may or may not be with me I still remember how once you weren't here at all
so I'd make up a mythical listener and there were good sides to that because I could choose
   myself

the degree of your presence the level of your attention from zero to fifty but then before I
   knew it
you were somehow actually with me though it's still a mystery as to why you decided to
   read me

but mystery or not in another before I knew it the make-believe between us had changed
to your not being with me because if I thought of you paying attention too closely you'd
   daunt me

This far along though all that's all over because if we're together or not if you're harking or not
we've had our times good and bad and with whom after all have I passed more intimate hours

with whom communed more to whom given over more of the secrets I swore when they
   barbed me
I'd keep to myself forever though I know now there's never forever and know too dear reader

here with me in one way or another that there aren't any mysteries I'd still care to conceal
so as long as you're out there nose in a book at your end of the page I'll keep scribbling at
   mine

Acknowledgments

Index of Titles

Index of First Lines

¿

Acknowledgments

Grateful acknowledgment is made to the editors of the following publications, where these poems, or versions of them, first appeared:

New England Review: "I Shot a Frog I Shot a Bird"

The New Republic: "Tears"

The New York Review of Books: "Dear Reader"

The New Yorker: "The Economy Rescued by My Mother Returning to Shop," "Hog"

Poetry East: "The Prick," "Smashed Nail"

Salmagundi: "Soul in Steel"

The Threepenny Review: "Mantis," "The Sun, the Saint, the Sot," "The World and Hokusai"

Times Literary Supplement: "Bark"

Tin House: "Little Hymn to Time"

Tweed: "At What Time on the Sabbath Do the Vultures Awake?"

Poem (UK): "Soul in Steel"

Index of Titles

Index of First Lines

Da Da Freud, Ma Ma Marx, growly Uncle Sartre—what a theory zoo to do your adolescence in, 210

Dear reader dearest inscrutable listener inscrutably harking or regrettably more likely not harking, 233

Don't make me tell it who's making me tell it why in the name of anything tell anything at all, 216

Even when the rain falls relatively hard, 33

Every morning of my life I sit at my desk getting whacked by some great poet or other, 143

Face powder, gunpowder, talcum of anthrax, 133

First I did my thing, that's to say her thing, to her, for her, 115

Her five horrid, deformed little dogs, who incessantly yap on the roof under my window, 3

Here was my relation with the woman who lived all last autumn and winter day and night, 22

"How do you say it? Cat-ah-reen?," 179

"I am dying of the itch," he thinks; a wheel jolts in a rut, the plank seat slaps at him, 189

I don't know what day or year of their secret cycle this blazing golden afternoon might be, 5

I hate how this unsummoned sigh-sound, sob-sound, 131

I keep rereading an article I found recently about how Mayan scribes, 75

I put my face inches from his, 56

I saw a spider on a library cornice snatch a plump, 80

I see they're tidying the Texas textbooks again, 147

I shot a frog, 222

I sleep as always these dark days aquiver I awake atremble my limbs jerk I thrash like a gaffed shark, 227

I was lugging my death from Kampala to Kraków, 120

I was walking home down a hill near our house on a balmy afternoon under the blossoms, 51

I wonder if any male but me is still living who remembers, 122

If that someone who's me yet not me yet who judges me is always with me, 93

If you were to possess a complicated, 113

In a certain town in New Jersey where now will be found malls car dealerships drive-throughs, 204

In the desert, a halo around the sun, a vast, prismed disk, **116**

In those days, those days which exist for me only as the most elusive memory now, **30**

It's coming at me again, damn, like that elephant with its schoonering ears charging in Uganda, **159**

Like a little boy with his daddy world takes Hokusai's hand to be led through the wilds of doubt, **203**

Many I could name but won't who'd have been furious to die while they were sleeping but did—, **165**

Maybe it's just my age, but sometimes these days when I'm making love to Catherine it feels, **180**

Men often find Catherine beautiful, and besides that the kind of beauty she has seems to make, **180**

My dream after the dream of more war: that for every brain, **127**

My grandson wants a *Ferrari*. I buy one for him. Why not?, **154**

My last god's a theodicy glutton, a good-evil gourmet—, **152**

Night, a wildly lashing deluge driving in great gusts over the blind, defeated fields, **10**

Not frail not fainthearted flighty and I certainly don't mean merely to mean unmale with those now, **201**

Not like a polar bear erupting from the water beside the edge of his glacier because as we, **206**

Not only have the skin and flesh and parts of the skeleton, **59**

Not so fast people were always telling me *Slow down take your time* teachers coaches, **158**

Often before have our fingers touched in sleep or half-sleep and enlaced, **26**

Often I have thought that after my death, not in death's void as we usually think it, **18**

Oh my, Harold Brodkey, of all people, after all this time appearing to me, **58**

Oh, sun, bright star, *our* star, dearest, nearest, how solacing you remain, how consoling your illuminations, **197**

On something like a plane he returns circling over rows of suburban monopoly houses, **123**

On the métro, I have to ask a young woman to move the packages beside her to make room for me, **97**

On the same tape, the two voices: the younger, pert, perky, so early on already suffused with, **171**

One branch, I read, of a species of chimpanzees has something like territorial wars, **118**

One more thing to keep, **63**

One of my grandsons is running through the park towards me to show me something he's, **193**

One of those great, garishly emerald flies that always look freshly generated from fresh excrement, **7**

One vast segment of the tree, the very topmost, blows ceremoniously against a breath of breeze, **38**

Only heartbreaking was it much later to first hear someone you loved speak of strangers with disdain, **61**

Raskolnikov hasn't slept. For days. In his brain, something like white, **136**

Saddening, worse, to read in "Frost at Midnight," **101**

Seven hundred tons per inch, I read, is the force in a bomb or shell in the microsecond after its detonation,
    103

She's magnificent, as we imagine women must be, **107**

Some days the best thing in a museum isn't the art, the paintings or statues, even those, say, **190**

Some dictator or other had gone into exile, and now reports were coming about his regime, **43**

Splendid that I'd revel even more in the butterflies harvesting pollen, **65**

Sweet to remember the tiny elevator I used to take to the garret someone had loaned me as an, **176**

Thank goodness we were able to wipe the Neanderthals out, beastly things, **156**

That astonishing thing that happens when you crack a needle awl into a block of ice, **25**

That dip in existence, that hollow, that falling-off place, cliff or abyss, **129**

That girl I didn't love, then because she was going to leave me, loved, **106**

That there is an entity, vast, omnipotent but immaterial, inaccessible to all human sense save hearing, **111**

The book goes fluttering crazily through the space of my room towards the wall like a bird, **9**

The heron methodically pacing like an old-time librarian down the stream through the patch, **170**

The horse trainer's horse is a scrawny pony; its ribs show, and when it levers itself onto its, **169**

The sexual terror lions are roaring into my ears as I make my way between their cages, **150**

The summer camp where I worked as a headwaiter when I was sixteen hired men off the Bowery, **174**

The way you'd renovate a ruined house, keeping the "shell," as we call it, brick, frame, or stone, **34**

The wide-bristled brooms that late at night in bus stations glide noiselessly over the terrazzo, **172**

There's no reserve, no hanging back in it, no thought of decorum, no thought of anything apparently, **179**

They hunted lions, they hunted humans, and enslaved them, 85

This time the holdup man didn't know a video-sound camera hidden up in a corner, 6

Three women old as angels, 46

Uncanny to realize one was *here*, so much, 66

Watch me, I'm running, watch me, I'm dancing, I'm air, 134

We'd wanted to make France, 27

Well here I, 39

What in the name of anything on earth was I doing crawling behind a billboard next to a bakery, 230

What must I do, to her, to myself, to believe or imagine I can believe in her? Ocher hills, I, 191

What was going through me at that time of childhood, 36

When Blackstone the magician cut a woman in half in the Branford theater, 132

When I offhandedly remarked to my father how sad it was that his good friend Sol would be, 192

When she walks our dog, Catherine tends to be a bit oblivious to how much mischief Bwindi, 183

When the Rothschilds were accumulating their vast fortunes, and even after, they wrote their, 187

When the workmen came to unclog the cesspool of the tiny house in Greece Catherine and I, 182

Where is it where is it where is it in what volume what text what treatise what tract, 87

Why this much fascination with you, little loves, why this what feels like, oh, hearts, 45

With *Fear and Trembling* I studied my Kierkegaard, with *Sickness unto Death*, 163

Wouldn't it be nice, I think, when the blue-haired lady in the doctor's waiting room bends over the magazine table, 42

Yesterday at four in the afternoon there were as accurately as I could count sixteen on fence posts, 218